The COUNTRY DIARY

CHRISTMAS
BOOK

also by Sarah Hollis

THE SHELL GUIDE TO THE
GARDENS OF ENGLAND
AND WALES

THE COUNTRY DIARY HERBAL

The Country Diary

CHRISTMAS
BOOK

Sarah Hollis

HENRY HOLT AND COMPANY

NEW YORK

Henry Holt and Company, Inc.
Publishers since 1866
115 West 18th Street
New York, New York 10011

Henry Holt ® is a registered
trademark of Henry Holt and Company, Inc.

First published in the United States in 1993 by
Henry Holt and Company, Inc.
Originally published in Great Britain in 1993 by
Michael Joseph Ltd.
The Penguin Group

Library of Congress Catalog Card Number: 93–78942

ISBN 0–8050–2925–7

Henry Holt books are available for special promotions and premiums.
For details contact: Director, Special Markets.

First American Edition—1993

Printed in England
All first editions are printed on acid-free paper. ∞

1 3 5 7 9 10 8 6 4 2

The publishers would like to thank Rowena Stott, Edith Holden's
great-niece and the owner of the original works, who has made the
publication of this book possible.

Title page picture: E. F. Skinner, Father Christmas

CONTENTS

Christmas card by Edith Holden

INTRODUCTION

This book is a celebration of the Edwardian Christmas, inspired by Edith Holden's famous books, *The Country Diary of an Edwardian Lady* and *Nature Notes of an Edwardian Lady*.

Christmas is the most loved of all our festivals, a time when families draw close and an air of generosity and goodwill abounds. Apart from its importance as a religious festival, the traditions that surround and enrich Christmas give it a timeless quality. This, though, is misleading, for much that we now think of as centuries old is relatively young, a marvellous inheritance from the Victorians who injected the festival with new vigour and colour. It was during this innovative and energetic period of our history that the Christmas tree was popularized, the harlequinade was transformed into the pantomime and ancient carols were rediscovered.

The Edwardians were fortunate indeed to live during a period that was known for its enjoyment of the good things of life. They were able to take advantage of their Victorian inheritance and at the same time put their own personal stamp on the festival. To feast at Christmas is traditional and the Edwardians, renowned for their gargantuan appetites and the generosity of their tables, would certainly not have stinted themselves. They also excelled at entertaining at home and were enthusiastic games players, so at Christmas there would have been no shortage of entertainment.

History is seldom tidy and to isolate the age purely to Edward VII's short reign from 1901 to 1910 would be misleading. It spilled over into Queen Victoria's monolithic reign and beyond Edward's, only to be cut short by the First World War. Most historians now consider the Edwardian age to date from 1880 to 1914 though, of course, no age is born or dies overnight but instead is gradually moulded and evolves under a plethora of both dramatic and subtle political, scientific, social and aesthetic influences.

Known as the 'Long Afternoon', the 'Golden Age' and the 'Indian Summer', the Edwardian age is chiefly remembered for the lavish and self-indulgent lifestyle of the upper classes, a class led by that most flamboyant of monarchs 'Good old Teddie' as the cockneys called him. But it was in fact a period of great contrasts. Beneath the thin upper crust of high society lay an expanding layer composed of the middle classes; and beneath that lurked the vast majority, the poor, who were still suffering from the low standards of a former age. They lived in appalling conditions, worked extraordinarily long hours and existed on pitiful wages.

But despite the poverty and lack of security for the working classes, an air of gaiety permeated the age from top to bottom. Could it have been because ale was twopence a pint and the Music Hall, cheap and always cheerful, was at the height of its popularity? Social observers now state that the nation sensed itself to be on the edge of an abyss and were making the most of the good things in life whilst they could. The First World War was certainly to change life radically and no family would be left untouched.

The period from the late nineteenth century up to the Great War which this book covers saw many exciting advances which offered new freedoms and opportunities to a wide span of society. There were new and popular modes of travel: the bicycle, as much used by women as men; the motorcar that first terrified, then entranced and revolutionized; and, most dramatic of all, the aeroplane. Only eight years after Queen Victoria's death in 1901, Bleriot successfully flew the Channel. Communications also saw mighty leaps forward, especially in 1901 when Marconi sent the first transatlantic radio signals from Cornwall to Newfoundland. In 1903 the Suffragette movement, the Women's Social and Political Union, was formed by Mrs Emmeline Pankhurst, her two daughters and the Oldham millworker, Annie Kenney. It was a movement that was to cause both social and political havoc.

It was certainly an age in which women were offered greater freedom, and Edith Holden, whose *Country Diary of an Edwardian Lady* and *Nature Notes of an Edwardian Lady* have inspired this book, was a young lady not atypical of her times. Born in 1871, she and her contemporaries might not have succeeded in acquiring the vote until after the First World War, but their lives were greatly affected and enlarged by the changing attitudes of their times. In her day it was considered worthwhile to give a girl a good, all-round education, even send her to university if she was so inclined. Energetic pursuits such as bicycling, tennis and hockey that the Victorians would have frowned upon were positively encouraged, and even a career was not considered out of the question.

Edith and her sisters were well educated at home, their mother Emma Wearing having been a governess before her marriage. Well read and artistic, they were encouraged to pursue their talents. After attending Birmingham School of Art, the best provincial art school in the country at that time, they went on to earn their living as artists and book illustrators.

Part of the new and thinking middle class, the Holden family – Edith, her parents, four sisters and two brothers – belonged to a section of society that did much to shape the Edwardian age. It was into families such as theirs that major political figures such as Asquith and Lloyd George were born, also scientists, writers, artists and architects. All of these joined together to sweep away many of the shortcomings of the Victorian age, its materialism, self righteousness and injustices. Trade unions and social movements such as the Fabians created a new awareness of working and living conditions, horse-drawn vehicles gradually gave way to motor buses and cars, newspapers and entertaining and specialist magazines proliferated, children's needs were catered for as never before and the nursery door was flung open. The Arts and Crafts Movement was superseded by Art Nouveau and Post-Impressionism, and garden cities which offered their inhabitants the best of both urban and rural life, were created. It was an exciting and fast-moving age.

A photograph of the Holden family in the late 1890s. Edith Holden is in the front row, third from the right, with her father Arthur Holden on her right

The light from the open door in Beatrix Potter's A Winter Scene – Hill Top, Sawrey *conjures up the conviviality and hospitality of a country home at Christmas*

The Holdens lived near Birmingham which was rapidly becoming the foremost manufacturing 'new' city of England as well as one of the cradles of social reform. Edith's father, Arthur Holden, was a member of the Unitarian Church, a Liberal and a radical who, as a respected member of the Birmingham Town Council, did much to improve the everyday living conditions of the city. The Holden children were certainly brought up to be aware of and help in a practical way those less fortunate than themselves – the invalid and slum children of Birmingham, for instance. In summer they would organize outings for them and at Christmas they staged magic lantern shows and produced a feast of mince pies and puddings.

What we know of the Holdens' lives gives us an idea of how such a family would have celebrated Christmas and woven into this book are many of Edith's thoughts, observations and charming illustrations. These contribute her own personal and characteristic enjoyment of the changing seasons and of Christmas itself. The Holdens were an inventive and artistic family, frequently welcomed friends to their home, enjoyed music, poetry and amateur dramatics and certainly had a sense of fun. This is demonstrated in an extract from a letter she wrote to the young Carol Trathen:

I hope you will all have a very merry Christmas all together; I shall think of you all and just wish I could pop in and see you for dinner-time on Christmas day. I should like to see you all dressed up in the paper caps etc. I was at a supper-party the other night; and we had crackers and every guest had a lovely bunch of violets placed by her seat. All the ladies put on their crowns and dunce's caps and mob-caps; one lady looked especially comic in a fire-man's helmet . . .

*We are all jogging along much as usual; next week we **shall** be busy; Mr and Mrs Heath are coming from London for a week; and very likely my friend Mr Smith [Edith married him in 1911] will be spending Christmas with us.*

The following chapters aim to bring the Edwardian Christmas alive through the writings and observation not only of Edith's own keen and artistic eye but also through those of many of her contemporaries. A good number would have shared a similar background and experiences and held the same attitudes, whilst others will paint a wider picture: a picture as richly filled as a plum pudding and one that mirrors the Edwardian age. Essentially the scene drawn reflects not the grandeur of the upper classes but the comfortable and unostentatious life of the Holden family. There are also suggestions for Christmas gifts, decorations and fare that can be made today. These are from the series of books inspired by Edith's *Country Diary* and *Nature Notes*.

The Edwardians certainly knew how to enjoy Christmas to the full. We might never enjoy their leisured lifestyle again, or live so cheaply on such a lavish scale, but we can relive the fun and excitement through their words and pictures and gain inspiration to enrich our own.

LANDMARKS OF THE EDWARDIAN ERA

January 1901: Queen Victoria dies.

December 1901: first Nobel Peace Prize.

May 1902: end of Boer War.

August 1902: Edward VII's Coronation.

September 1902: reliability trials from Crystal Palace to Folkestone for the Automobile Club.

December 1902: Beatrix Potter's *The Tale of Peter Rabbit* is published.

1902: seven telephone exchanges operating in London.

December 1903: first garden city, Letchworth, Herts, is built: a town for 30,000 people, marrying best of rural and urban life.

1904: reliable light cars for sale from £150. First Motor Car act – cars were not allowed to exceed 20 m.p.h.

13 December 1904: first electric train left Baker Street for Uxbridge.

January 1905: first Suffragettes were sent to prison – Christabel and Emmeline Pankhurst.

1906: Bakerloo and Piccadilly underground opened.

February 1906: W.S. Kellogg forms Battle Creek Toasted Cornflake Co. to make the cereal he invented as therapy for mental patients.

December 1907: Nobel Prize for Literature goes to Kipling.

December 1908: first performance of the play of *The Wind in the Willows*.

1909: Bleriot flies the Channel.

1909: first old age pensions drawn.

1909: Selfridges opens – six acres of departments, classed as 'American' store.

1910: Edward VII dies.

1910: transatlantic wireless service begins.

1912: Morris Oxford Car is manufactured.

1912: National coal strike.

January 1912: Scott beaten to the Pole.

April 1912: *Titanic* sinks.

February 1913: Scott and his party found dead.

October 1913: Panama Canal opened.

1913: Suffragettes wage a more violent campaign.

June 1914: Archduke Ferdinand assassinated.

August 1914: Britain declares war.

CHRISTMAS COUNTRYSIDE

A lthough the countryside at Christmas is de-nuded of its spring and summer finery, it has a subtle beauty and colouring all its own and the handsome 'bone structure' of the landscape and naked trees is highlighted. The flowers that have the courage to make an appearance at this time are doubly appreciated for being sparse and frequently have the sweetest scents of all. Wildlife in general is shy, but the bitterly cold months are a time when many birds, if offered food, can be observed at close quarters. Edith was a country girl at heart and enjoyed to the full all that it had to offer. The Holdens were fortunate in always finding a home in rural surroundings within commuting distance of Birmingham. Far from being simply a fair-weather observer and artist of flora and fauna, she would venture out on foot or on her bicycle to visit old haunts as well as make new discoveries. The relatively slow pace of Edwardian life enabled her to obey the bidding of W. H. Henry Davies who urged us in his poem 'Leisure' to '. . . *stand beneath the boughs/And stare as long as sheep or cows.'*

In such a way did Edith absorb the shy colouring, varied textures and shapes of the countryside, so as to be able to translate them onto paper on her return home.

The gardens of the various houses owned by the Holdens also provided her with an opportunity to observe birdlife at close quarters on a daily basis, as well as cultivate and appreciate the unique qualities of flowers throughout the seasons.

The vagaries of the weather and its effects on the landscape and wildlife were also noted in Edith's diary, and it is not difficult to sense a thrill of excitement on her discovering the snow on Christmas morning 1906. A white Christmas is a rare event and seems to complete so perfectly the celebrations.

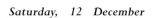

The bare skeletons of trees, in all their variety, from ancient twisted oaks to spreading beeches, are a majestic sight in winter and one admired both by Edith and the Revd Francis Kilvert. Kilvert, though not an artist, was able to paint lively word pictures in his diary, not only of his everyday life as a priest, but also of the natural world he saw about him. Frequently humorous and often poignant, the style and content resemble that of letters to a friend, rather than a dry account of facts. In charge of a rural parish he, like a country doctor, had to go out in all weathers to visit his parishioners in trouble, and consequently he saw the countryside in all its different guises.

Saturday, 12 December
There is a beauty in the trees peculiar to winter, when their fair delicate slender tracery unveiled by leaves and showing clearly against the sky rises bending with a lofty arch or sweeps gracefully drooping. The crossing and interlacing of the limbs, the smaller boughs and tender twigs make an exquisitely fine network which has something of the severe beauty of sculpture, while the tree in summer in its full pride and splendour and colour of foliage represents the loveliness of painting. The deciduous trees which seem to me most graceful and elegant in winter are the birches, limes, beeches. ■
FRANCIS KILVERT,
DIARY 1870–1879

Dec. 14. **Heavy fall of snow.**

Dec. 20. **After a rapid thaw and four days of wonderfully mild, still weather, without wind or rain, the wind has gone round to the east and it looks as if we might have a frosty Christmas after all.**

Dec. 25. **We woke to a snowy Christmas morning, sunshine later and sharp frost at night.**

Dec. 26. **Another heavy fall of snow in the night.**

Dec. 27. **In the paper today it reports that all Britain lies under snow from John o'Groats to Land's End for the first time for six years.**

COUNTRY DIARY

Claude Monet, The Magpie

Francis Thompson, who died in 1907, might well have been inspired by that very same white Christmas to write the following poem. Who has not looked closely at a snowflake and wondered at its miraculous intricacy?

TO A SNOWFLAKE

What heart could have thought you? –
Past our devisal
(O filigree petal!)
Fashioned so purely,
Fragilely, surely,
From what Paradisal
Imagineless metal,
Too costly for cost?
Who hammered you, wrought you,
From argentine vapour?
'God was my shaper.
Passing surmisal,
He hammered, He wrought me,
From curled silver vapour,
To lust of His mind:
Thou could'st not have thought me!
So purely, so palely,
Tinily, surely,
Mightily, frailly,
Insculped and embossed,
With His hammer of wind,
And His graver of frost.'

FRANCIS THOMPSON

LETTER FROM VIRGINIA WOOLF

25 December 1906 It has been quite an absurd Christmas Day – I think – I was woken by sunlight dancing on my nose, and cursed, and woke and saw the whole pane blue, and then the whole field white, and little birds and modest cottages, and blue smoke and peaceful trees: I should have saluted the happy morn had I been a Christian. As it was I went and knocked up Adrian and we came down to our letters and parcels. Then in the intervals of eating turkey we have tramped the forest, which is as painted wood, all clear sharp tints, and delicate lines, and crisp white spaces . . . And then we sat and read. ■

LETTER FROM VIRGINIA WOOLF
TO VIOLET DICKENSON

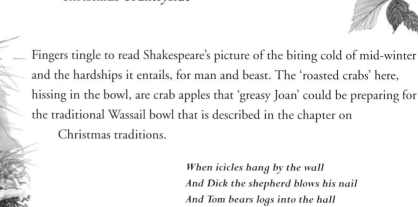

Fingers tingle to read Shakespeare's picture of the biting cold of mid-winter and the hardships it entails, for man and beast. The 'roasted crabs' here, hissing in the bowl, are crab apples that 'greasy Joan' could be preparing for the traditional Wassail bowl that is described in the chapter on Christmas traditions.

When icicles hang by the wall
And Dick the shepherd blows his nail
And Tom bears logs into the hall
And milk comes frozen home in pail
When blood is nipped and ways be foul,
Then nightly sings the staring owl,
To-whit!
To-who! – a merry note;
While greasy Joan doth keel the pot.

When all aloud the wind doth blow
And coughing drowns the parson's saw,
And birds sit brooding in the snow,
And Marian's nose looks red and raw.
When roasted crabs hiss in the bowl
Then nightly sings the staring owl,
To-whit!
To-who! – a merry note,
While greasy Joan doth keel the pot.
WILLIAM SHAKESPEARE

The beauty of the day was of itself sufficient to inspire philanthropy. Notwithstanding the frostiness of the morning, the sun in his cloudless journey had acquired sufficient power to melt away the thin covering of snow from every southern declivity, and to bring out the living green which adorns an English landscape even in mid-winter. Large tracts of smiling verdure contrasted with the dazzling whiteness of the shaded slopes and hollows. Every sheltered bank, on which the broad rays rested, yielded its silver rill of cold and limpid water, glittering through the dripping grass; and sent up slight exhalations to contribute to the thin haze that hung just above the surface of the earth. There was something truly cheering in this triumph of warmth and verdure over the frosty thraldom of winter; it was, as the squire observed, an emblem of Christmas hospitality, breaking through the chills of ceremony and selfishness, and thawing every heart into a flow. He pointed with pleasure to the indications of good cheer reeking from the chimneys of the comfortable farmhouses, and low thatched cottages. 'I love,' said he, 'to see this day well kept by rich and poor; it is a great thing to have one day in the year, at least, when you are sure of being welcome wherever you go, and of having, as it were, the world all thrown open to you.' ■
WASHINGTON IRVING, *SKETCH BOOK*

The snow seldom lingers for long in Britain and as it melts the colouring of the gradually revealed fields is emphasized. A walk on Christmas day such as that taken by Washington Irving with his host, the squire, always has a leisured quality about it. The 'business' of the world draws to a halt and everyone, both rich and poor, enjoys a sense of universal goodwill.

from THE COTTAGER

He is a simple-worded plain old man
Whose good intents take errors in their plan.

And many a moving tale in antique rhymes
He has for Christmas and such merry times,
When 'Chevy Chase', his masterpiece of song,
Is said so earnest none can think it long...
In an old corner cupboard by the wall
His books are laid, though good, in number small,
His Bible first in place;...
And prayer-book next, much worn though strongly bound,
Prove him a churchman orthodox and sound.
The Pilgrim's Progress** and the **Death of Abel
Are seldom missing from his Sunday table...

Far from his cottage door in peace or strife
He ne'er went fifty miles in all his life.
His knowledge with old notions still combined
Is twenty years behind the march of mind.

Life gave him comfort but denied him wealth,
He toils in quiet but enjoys his health...

JOHN CLARE

Birket Foster, Winter – Cottage in Snow and
Sunset

Although John Clare wrote the above a good seventy years before
the Edwardian era, the life of the cottager he describes differed little from
that of Edith's day. For many from rural districts, joining up during the First
World War and going to France was an extraordinary adventure, for
they, like the cottager in the poem, had not travelled even
fifty miles from their homes.

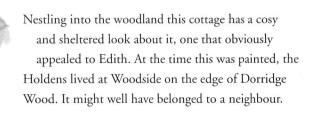

Nestling into the woodland this cottage has a cosy
and sheltered look about it, one that obviously
appealed to Edith. At the time this was painted, the
Holdens lived at Woodside on the edge of Dorridge
Wood. It might well have belonged to a neighbour.

The shepherd, as opposed to the farmer, has a far harder time of it living outdoors night and day with his flock and his dog. *A Shepherd's Life*, written by W. H. Hudson in 1910, describes the hardships suffered and, drawing on the life of one particular shepherd, paints a lively picture of the sort of character that can withstand such a lonely life. There could be no Christmas break for him, especially if it snowed.

Joseph Farquharson, Glowed with Tints of Evening Hours

He agreed that it was very quiet on the downs, and that he loved their quiet. 'Fifty years,' he said, 'I've been on the downs and the fields, day and night, seven days a week, and I've been told that it's a poor way to spend a life, working seven days for ten or twelve, or at most thirteen shillings. But I never seen it like that; I liked it, and I always did my best. You see, sir, I took a pride in it. I never left a place but I was asked to stay. When I left it was because of something I didn't like. I couldn't never abide cruelty to a dog or any beast. And I couldn't abide bad language. If my master swore at the sheep or the dog I wouldn't abide with he – no, not for a pound a week. I liked my work, and I liked knowing things about the sheep. Not things in books, for I never had no books, but what I found out with my own sense, if you can understand me.'

After our long Sunday talk we were silent for a time, and then he uttered these impressive words: 'I don't say that I want to have my life again, because 'twould be sinful. We must take what is sent. But if 'twas offered to me and I was told to choose my work, I'd say, Give me my Wiltsheer Downs again and let me be a shepherd there all my life long.' ∎

W.H. HUDSON, *A SHEPHERD'S LIFE*

The lot of the farmer is easier in some respects at Christmas time since his livestock is gathered in during the harsh winter months. Seeing the animals in the barns at this time of the year conjures up pictures in the mind of how the stable must have looked when Christ was born. Thomas Hardy was a true countryman and also imagined that scene, set, not in Bethlehem, but in his beloved Dorset.

THE OXEN

Christmas Eve, and twelve of the clock
'Now they are all on their knees,'
An elder said as we sat in a flock
By the embers in hearthside ease.

We pictured the meek mild creatures where
They dwelt in their strawy pen,
Nor did it occur to one of us there
To doubt they were kneeling then.

So fair a fancy few would weave
In these years! Yet, I feel,
If someone said on Christmas Eve,
'Come; see the oxen kneel

'In the lonely barton by yonder coomb
Our childhood used to know,'
I should go with him in the gloom,
Hoping it might be so.
THOMAS HARDY

A WINTER PIECE

And yet but lately have I seen, e'en here,
The Winter in a lovely dress appear.

For ev'ry shrub, and ev'ry blade of grass,
And ev'ry pointed thorn, seem'd wrought in glass,
In pearls and rubies rich the hawthorns show,
While thro' the ice the crimson berries glow;
The thick-sprung reeds the watry marshes yield,
Seem polish'd lances in a hostile field,
The stag in limpid currents with surprize
Sees chrystal branches on his forehead rise.
The spreading oak, the beech, and tow'ring pine,
Glaz'd over, in the freezing aether shine.
The frighted birds the rattling branches shun,
That wave and glitter in the distant sun.
When if a sudden gust of wind arise,
The brittle forest into atoms flies:
The crackling wood beneath the tempest bends,
And in a spangled show'r the prospect ends.
AMBROSE PHILIPS

Beatrix Potter, Sawrey from Tower Bank Arms

It is not surprising that the robin with his cheerful 'ruddy vest' became a wildlife symbol of Christmas and the favourite of Christmas card manufacturers. Of all the wild birds he is the most bold and friendly at this time of year. Throughout the year but especially in winter he is the gardener's friend, on the look-out for any worms that might appear as the ground is turned.

Jan. 26. The last few weeks, our own and our neighbours' gardens have been haunted by a very curious Robin. The whole of the upper plumage, which in ordinary Robins is brown, shaded with olive green, is light silvery grey in this bird, so that when flying about it looks like a white bird with a scarlet breast. I hear that it was seen about here last summer, it is so conspicuous, it is a wonder it has not fallen a victim to somebody's gun. ■

COUNTRY DIARY

THE ROBIN

Art thou the bird whom man loves best,
The pious bird with the scarlet breast,
Our little English robin;
The bird that comes about our doors
When autumn winds are sobbing?
The bird who by some name or other
All men who know thee call their brother?
　　　　WILLIAM WORDSWORTH

Lucien Pissarro, Ivy Cottage,
Coldharbour, Sun and Snow

Harriett M. Bennett, The First
Robin

THE ROBIN

I love the lark that cleaves the morning skies
And that inspired recluse the nightingale
I love the wandering voice that cuckoo cries
And doves that plead anon in beechen vale

I love the throstle whistling in the rain,
And golden-bill a-carol on the thorn;
And many a treble pipe and lilting strain
That comes with spring and revels in the dawn

But oh, when all the red and russet fires
Have waned at last along the woodland way
How fresh and clear amid the ruined choirs
The wild, sweet snatches of the robin's lay

Trim-suited bard! – beneath that ruddy vest
The lyric soul of music surely lives.
And as it takes with storm his tiny breast
He little knows the joy to me he gives;

But hops away amid the matted leaves
His beady eyes as black as shining jet,
While still with tears the stricken forest grieve
Whose every bough is hung with jewels wet.

He is the friend of yon secluded cot.
And when the wood is wreathed in wintry snows
Full many a crumb from no unstinted lot
The labourer's wife to Robin Redbreast throws

And though mid hardy frost he scarce may sing
When surly fiends the very streams congeal
And o'er the wold, the storm on scudding wing
Bids every lesser bird himself conceal.

Yet soon once more from some sequestered nook
Of rambling barn or overhanging reef,
Or ivied bank beside the running brook
He drops as lightly as a withered leaf

And sings again the song we ne'er despise
Yet scarce remember mid o'erwhelming fate; –
Of secret Joy – that never wholly dies
Nor is less sweet because the spring is late. . .

NATURE NOTES

Putting out food for the birds in winter near the house can create a new source of entertainment. The pecking order, bullying, courage or timidity of the different species – size not being the major factor – is fascinating to watch. There is excitement, too, when a new, and seldom seen, visitor makes its appearance.

By Christmas berries in the wild and in the garden are scarce and one is hard pressed to find holly, somehow ignored by the birds, that still bears an abundance. The birds are not so partial to those of the privet and ivy, and cotoneasters in the garden manage to retain their warm glow.

There are some birds which are purely winter visitors to these islands, arriving in the Autumn and leaving for more northern lands with the approach of spring. Such among the smaller birds are the Fieldfare, Redwing; Mountain finch, Snow-Bunting, Grosbeak and Grey Shrike. These birds never or rarely breed in Britain. The Field-fare and Redwing nest in the large birch and pine forests of Sweden and Norway. These countries as well as Iceland, Lapland and Russia are the summer home of the Snow-bunting and Mountain Finch, while the Gros-beak and Grey Shrike are also met with in North America. The two latter birds are very rare in England.

Birds of all kinds are to be seen going about in large flocks in the winter months, traversing the fields in search of food. Among the birds who thus congregate together are – Rooks, Wild Pigeons, Plovers, Missel thrushes, Field-fares, Red-wings, Starlings, Sparrows, Buntings, Larks, Finches of all kinds Tits, and Golden-crested Wrens. The Tits and Gold-crests may often be seen going about the larch trees in company. The latter are much more common than is generally supposed; but they frequent pine and fir woods and seldom go near dwelling-houses. Though retiring in their habits they will allow themselves to be approached quite closely when busily employed running over the twigs in their search for insects. ■

NATURE NOTES

Dec. 1. Very bright and clear with a cold wind from the north east. For many weeks past the birds have been coming to be fed in the mornings. Today I put out a cocoa-nut, to the great joy of the Tom-tits, numbers of them were pecking away at it all through the day – mostly Blue-tits.

Dec. 4. Three days of rain, wind and sunshine.

Dec. 7. Hard white frost and fog. This is the first real winter's day we have had. Crowds of birds came to be fed this morning. There were great battles among the Tits over the cocoa-nut; and once a Robin got right into it and refused to let the Tits approach, until he had had all he wanted. I don't think the Robins really care for cocoa-nut; but they don't like to see the Tits enjoying anything, without claiming a share.

COUNTRY DIARY

Anon, Young Boy with Birds in Snow (*postcard*)

Weather forecast for London and Channel unsettled, sleet showers. ■

DAILY CHRONICLE,
25 DECEMBER 1906

Mrs C. W. Earle's book *Pot Pourri from a Surrey Garden* was a run-away bestseller when it was published in 1897. Written as a diary, it was full of down-to-earth advice for the lady of the house regarding decoration, food and the garden, as well as tips on how to bring up daughters. She puts her feelings about the country-side so well when she says, 'I love the country in winter; one expects nothing and everything is a joy and a surprise.' She was enchanted by the sight of the first, delicate winter aconite in her garden, a flower that Vita Sackville-West described thus:

Hardly anything grows here to perfection when left alone. Most plants require either chalk, peat, leaf-mould or cow-manure, and half-tender things are now the better for covering up with matting or Bracken-fern. It is seldom of any use to come so early as this; but there has been no cold this year, though one feels it must come. Oh! such days and days of gloom and darkness; but today the wind freshened from the north-east, and I could breathe once more. How delightful it is to be out of London again! There is always plenty to do and to enjoy. How the birds sing, as if it were spring! I love the country in winter; one expects nothing, and everything is a joy and a surprise. The Freesias are flowering well; they improve each year as the bulbs get larger. Cyclamens are in the greenhouse, and a large, never-failing, old white Azalea, which forces faithfully and uncomplainingly every year, and from which we cut so many blooms.

The first Aconite! Does any flower in summer give the same pleasure? The blue-green blades of the Daffodils and Jonquils are firmly and strongly pushing through the cold brown earth; nothing in all the year gives such a sense of power and joy. ■

MRS C.W. EARLE,
POT POURRI FROM A SURREY GARDEN

from THE GARDEN

The winter aconite with mint
* of gold*
Like new-struck coins that shame
* the spectral sun*
Hung in our jaundiced heaven,
* — these are frail,*
So frail it seems they scarcely
* could endure*
One touch of horrid life and
* life's fierce wind.*
VITA SACKVILLE-WEST

In these days of central heating how many readers will remember the entrancing patterns made by frost on the window panes – a fantasy world which the Edwardians must frequently have enjoyed on bedroom or nursery window, but which is a rarity today.

I will sing praises unto my God while I have any being. Ps. 146.2.

And we should pass along
the earth,
Like birds that live upon
the wing;
Rise to the country of our birth,
And on our way its anthems sing.
FOR THE MASTER'S SAKE

As an invalid, the writer Katherine Mansfield found joy in watching the birds from her window. Birdsong in the depths of winter always holds a promise of the spring to come – a happy thought to those unwillingly confined indoors.

Little round birds in the fir tree at the side window, scouring the tree for food. I crumbled a piece of bread but though the crumbs fell in the branches only two found them. There was a strange remoteness in the air, the scene, the winter cheeping. In the evening, for the first time for – I felt rested. I sat up in bed and discovered I was singing within. Even the sound of the wind is different. It is joyful, not ominous. ■

KATHERINE MANSFIELD, *LETTERS AND JOURNALS 1888–1923*

JOHN FROST

The door was shut, as doors should be,
Before you went to bed last night,
Yet John Frost has got in, you see,
And left your windows silver white. . .

And now you cannot see the trees
Nor fields that stretch beyond the lane;
But there are fairer things than these
His fingers traced on every pane.

Rocks and castles towering high,
Hills and dales, and streams and fields,
And knights in armour riding by
With plumes and spears and shining shields.

And here are little boats, and there
Big ships with sails spread to the breeze
And yonder palm-trees, waving fair
On islands set in silver seas.

And butterflies with gauzy wings,
And birds and bees, and cows and sheep,
And fruit and flowers, and all the things
You see when you are sound asleep.

For, creeping softly underneath
The door when all the lights are out,
John Frost takes every breath you breathe,
And knows the things you think about.

He paints them on the window-pane,
In fairy lines, with frozen steam;
And when you wake, you see again
The wondrous things you saw in dream.

ANON

Christmas roses were also a favourite of the great Edwardian gardener Gertrude Jekyll, who did so much to transform the stiff and pompous Victorian garden into one that flattered rather than tortured nature. She also extols the virtues of the startling blue *Iris stylosa* (now known as the *Iris unguicularis*) which looks so fragile that it is hard to believe it will survive a day in the cold. A small vase of these in bleak mid-winter never fails to draw comment and reminds one of summer.

Ere doth the floral pageant close
With one last flower –
a Christmas Rose.

∞ The End. ∞

The graceful Christmas rose fairy was probably drawn by well-known book illustrator Walter Crane, who was a patron of the Birmingham School of Art attended by Edith and her sisters.

Christmas Roses keep on flowering bravely, in spite of our light soil and frequent summer drought, both being unfavourable conditions; but bravest of all is the blue Algerian Iris (*Iris stylosa*), flowering freely as it does, at the foot of a west wall, in all open weather from November till April.

I never tire of admiring and praising *Iris stylosa*, which has proved itself such a good plant for English gardens; at any rate, for those in our southern counties. Lovely in form and colour, sweetly-scented and with admirable foliage, it has in addition to these merits the unusual one of a blooming season of six months' duration. The first flowers come with the earliest days of November, and its season ends with a rush of bloom in the first half of April. Then is the time to take up old tufts and part them, and plant afresh; the old roots will have dried up into brown wires, and the new will be pushing. It thrives in rather poor soil, and seems to bloom all the better for having its root-run invaded by some stronger plant. When I first planted a quantity I had brought from its native place, I made the mistake of putting it in a well-prepared border. At first I was delighted to see how well it flourished, but as it gave me only thick masses of leaves a yard long, and no flowers, it was clear that it wanted to be less well fed. After changing it to poor soil, at the foot of a sunny wall close to a strong clump of Alströmeria, I was rewarded with a good crop of flowers; and the more the Alströmeria grew into it on one side and *Plumbago Larpentæ* on the other, the more freely the brave little Iris flowered. The flower has no true stem; what serves as a stem, sometimes a foot long, is the elongated tube, so that the seed-pod has to be looked for deep down at the base of the tufts of leaves, and almost under ground. The specific name, *stylosa*, is so clearly descriptive, that one regrets that the longer, and certainly uglier, *unguicularis* should be preferred by botanists. ■

GERTRUDE JEKYLL,
WOOD AND GARDEN

Vita Sackville-West also wrote about that most rewarding of winter flowering plants, the Christmas rose, and offered advice on its cultivation. What could be more satisfying for the gardener than to raise a few of these for the festive season?

The Christmas roses, *Helleborus niger*, are in flower now. They don't like being moved – in gardening language, they 'resent disturbance' – so even if you will take my advice and plant some clumps in early spring, which is the best time to move them, directly after they have finished flowering you may have to wait a year or two before they begin to reward you with their green-white flowers and their golden centres. They are worth waiting for, believe me.

They like a rather shady place; moist but well drained. A western aspect suits them. Once planted, leave them alone. They will grow in strength from year to year. I have a plant in my garden which to my certain knowledge has been there for fifty years. It was bequeathed to me by an old country-woman of the old type, who wanted me to have the enjoyment of it after she had gone. ■

VITA SACKVILLE-WEST,
VITA SACKVILLE-WEST'S GARDEN BOOK

City-dwellers doubly appreciate the unexpected or bold appearance of nature in urban surroundings – the wild flower that has somehow seeded itself between paving stones and survived – and a freak snowfall. That described below stops them literally and metaphorically in their tracks, provides a delightful diversion from the daily grind and creates a sense of wonder. For a day or two the natural world dictates every move.

Christmas card painted by one of the Holden family

LONDON SNOW

When men were all asleep the snow came flying,
In large white flakes falling on the city brown,
Stealthily and perpetually settling and loosely lying,
Hushing the latest traffic of the drowsy town;

Deadening, muffling, stifling its murmurs failing;
Lazily and incessantly floating down and down:
Silently sifting and veiling road, roof and railing;
Hiding difference, making unevenness even,
Into angles and crevices softly drifting and sailing.
All night it fell, and when full inches seven
It lay in the depth of its uncompacted lightness,
The clouds blew off from a high and frosty heaven;
And all woke earlier for the unaccustomed brightness
Of the winter dawning, the strange unheavenly glare:
The eye marvelled – marvelled at the dazzling whiteness;
The ear hearkened to the stillness of the solemn air;
No sound of wheel rumbling nor of foot falling,
And the busy morning cries came thin and spare.
Then boys I heard, as they went to school, calling,
They gathered up the crystal manna to freeze

Their tongues with tasting, their hands with snowballing;
Or rioted in a drift, plunging up to the knees;
Or peering up from under the white-mossed wonder,
'O look at the trees!' they cried, 'O look at the trees!'
With lessened load a few carts creak and blunder,
Following along the white deserted way,
A country company long dispersed asunder:
When now already the sun, in pale display
Standing by Paul's high dome, spread forth below
His sparkling beams, and awoke the stir of the day.
For now doors open, and war is waged with the snow;
And trains of sombre men, past tale of number,
Tread long brown paths, as toward their toil they go;

But even for them awhile no cares encumber
Their minds diverted; the daily word is unspoken,
The daily thoughts of labour and sorrow slumber
At the sight of the beauty that greets them, for the charm they
have broken.

ROBERT BRIDGES

TOY HEDGEHOG

Size
Approximate length 30cm,
11¾ins

Materials
3 × 50g balls Emu Superwash DK in
main colour (M)
1 ball contrast colour (C)
One pair 5mm (US8) knitting needles
Oddment (odds and ends) of black yarn
for eyes and nose
Small piece of black felt for paws
Stuffing

Tension / Gauge
14 sts and 22 rows to 10cm, 4ins over
fur stitch using 5mm (US8) needles
and yarn double
N.B. Use yarn double throughout

FUR STITCH
1st row: (RS) K1, ☆K1 but do not
drop st off left needle, bring yarn
forward between needles and wind
over left thumb to form a loop
approximately 4cm, 1½ins, take yarn
between needles to back and K the
same st again but this time drop st off
left needle, bring yarn forward
between needles then take it over right
needle to make a loop, pass the 2 sts
just knitted over this loop and off right
needle, K next st☆, rep from ☆ to ☆
to last 2 sts, K2.
2nd row: K.
3rd row: K2, rep from ☆ to ☆ of 1st
row to last st, K1.
4th row: K.
These 4 rows form fur stitch.

LEFT BACK
Beg at rear end.
Using 5mm (US8) needles and M, cast
on 7 sts.
Working in fur stitch throughout and
taking care to keep patt correct, shape
work thus:

1st row: Work to end.
2nd row: Inc 1 st at each end of row.
3rd row: Inc 1st at beg of row.
4th row: Inc 1 st at beg of row.
5th row: Inc 1 st at each end of row.
6th row: Work to end.
7th and 8th rows: As 5th and 6th rows.
9th row: As 3rd row.
10th row: Work to end.
11th row: Inc 1 st at beg of row and
dec 1 st at end of row.
12th–14th rows: Work to end.
15th–18th rows: As 11th–14th rows.
19th and 20th rows: As 11th and 12th
rows.
21st row: Inc 1 st at end of row.
22nd row: Work to end.
23rd–26th rows: As 21st and 22nd
rows.
27th row: As 21st row.
28th row: Inc 1st at beg of row.
29th–34th rows: As 27th and 28th
rows.
35th–37th rows: Work to end.

Although the hedgehog hibernates during the
winter, children playing in the garden
can come across them buried
beneath a pile of leaves
– or, of course,
in this
form, at the
bottom of their
Christmas stockings.

Christmas day is the time when new hats, scarves and gloves are donned against the cold and taken out on a walk in the countryside. These robin jumpers and the little boy's hat and scarf would not only make perfect gifts but also be ideal for such an outing.

ROBIN MAN'S AND BOY'S SWEATERS

Sizes

To fit chest 56 – 61[66 – 71:76 – 81:86 – 91:97 – 102:107 – 112]cm, 22 – 24[26 – 28:30 – 32:34 – 36:38 – 40:42 – 44]ins

Actual chest 69[80:91:102.5:114: 125]cm, $27\frac{1}{4}$[$31\frac{1}{2}$:36:$40\frac{1}{4}$:45:$49\frac{1}{4}$]ins

Length 38.5[46:54:61:64:68]cm, $15\frac{1}{4}$[$18\frac{1}{4}$:$21\frac{1}{2}$:24:$25\frac{1}{4}$:$26\frac{3}{4}$]ins

Sleeve seam 30[36:42:46:48:49]cm, $11\frac{3}{4}$[$14\frac{1}{4}$:$16\frac{1}{2}$:$18\frac{1}{4}$:19:$19\frac{1}{4}$]ins

Materials

4[5:6:7:8:9] × 100g balls of Samband Lopi

One pair each $4\frac{1}{2}$mm (US7) and $6\frac{1}{2}$mm (US10$\frac{1}{2}$) knitting needles

Cable needle

Tension / Gauge

14 sts and 19 rows to 10cm, 4ins over st st using $6\frac{1}{2}$mm (US10$\frac{1}{2}$) needles

BACK

☆☆Using $4\frac{1}{2}$mm (US7) needles, cast on 42[52:56:64:72:80] sts.

Cont in K1, P1 rib for 5[5:7:7:7:7]cm,

$2[2:2\frac{3}{4}:2\frac{3}{4}:2\frac{3}{4}]$ins, ending with a RS row.

Inc. row: Rib 7[8:6:10:8:7], ☆inc in next st, rib 3[4:3:3:4:5], rep from ☆ to last 7[9:6:10:9:7] sts, inc in next st, rib to end. 50[60:68:76:84:92] sts.

Change to $6\frac{1}{2}$mm (US10$\frac{1}{2}$) needles and commence patt.

1st size only

1st row: (RS) Sl 1, (K5, P2) 3 times, K6, (P2, K5) 3 times, K1 tbl.

2nd row: Sl 1, (P5, K2) 3 times, P6, (K2, P5) 3 times, K1 tbl.

3rd–6th rows: Rep 1st–2nd rows twice.

7th row: Sl 1, (K5, P2) 3 times, sl next 3 sts onto cable needle and hold at back of work, K3 then K3 from cable needle – called C6B, (P2, K5) 3 times, K1 tbl.

8th row: As 2nd row.

9th–12th rows: Rep 1st–2nd rows twice.

These 12 rows form the patt.

2nd, 3rd, 4th, 5th and 6th sizes only

1st row: (RS) Sl 1, K[2:6:10:14:18], P2, K6, (P2, K5) twice, P2, K6, P2, (K5, P2) twice, K6, P2, K[2:6:10:14:18], K1 tbl.

2nd row: Sl 1, P[2:6:10:14:18], K2, P6, (K2, P5) twice, K2, P6, K2, (P5, K2) twice, P6, K2, P[2:6:10:14:18], K1, tbl.

3rd–6th rows: Rep 1st–2nd rows twice.

7th row: Sl 1, K[2:6:10:14:18], P2, C6B– see 1st size, (P2, K5) twice, P2, C6B, P2, (K5, P2) twice, C6B, P2, K[2:6:10:14:18], K1 tbl.

8th row: As 2nd row.

9th–12th rows: Rep 1st–2nd rows twice.

These 12 rows form the patt.

All sizes

Cont in patt until work measures

24[30:35:39:41:43]cm, $9\frac{1}{2}$[12:13$\frac{3}{4}$: 15$\frac{1}{2}$:16:17]ins from beg, ending with a WS row.

Shape armholes

Dec 1 st at each end of every row until 38[48:54:62:68:76] sts rem.☆☆

Cont without further shaping until work measures 38.5[46:54:61: 64:68]cm, 15$\frac{1}{4}$ [18$\frac{1}{4}$:21$\frac{1}{4}$:24:25$\frac{1}{4}$: 26$\frac{3}{4}$]ins from beg, ending with a WS row.

Shape shoulders

Cast off 5[6:8:9:9:11] sts at beg of next 2 rows, then 6[7:8:9:10:11] sts at beg of foll 2 rows. Leave rem 16[22:22:26:30:32] sts on a spare needle.

FRONT

Work as given for back from ☆☆ to ☆☆. Cont without further shaping until work measures 33[41:47:55:58:61]cm, 13[16:18$\frac{1}{2}$:21 $\frac{3}{4}$:22$\frac{3}{4}$:24]ins from beg, ending with a WS row.

Shape neck

Next row: Patt 15[19:22:24:25:28] and turn, leaving rem sts on a spare needle.

Complete left side of neck first.

Dec 1 st at neck edge on every row until 13[15:19:21:21:24] sts rem, then on every foll alt row until 11[13:16:18:19:22] sts rem. Cont without further shaping until work measures same as back to shoulder shaping, ending at armhole edge.

Shape shoulder

Cast off 5[6:8:9:9:11] sts at beg of next row. Work 1 row. Cast off rem 6[7:8:9:10:11] sts.

With RS of work facing, return to sts on spare needle. Sl centre 8[10:10:14:18:20] sts onto a holder, rejoin yarn at neck edge, patt to end.

Complete to match first side of neck.

SLEEVES

Using $4\frac{1}{2}$mm (US7) needles, cast on 20[24:28:30:34:38] sts.

Cont in K1, P1 rib for 5[5:7:7:7:7]cm, $2[2:2\frac{3}{4}:2\frac{3}{4}:2\frac{3}{4}:2\frac{3}{4}]$ins, ending with a RS row.

Inc row: Rib 5[4:3:6:3:5], ☆ inc in next st, rib 1[2:2:1:2:2], rep from ☆ to last 5[5:4:6:4:6] sts, inc in next st, rib to end. 26[30:36:40:44:48] sts.

Change to $6\frac{1}{2}$mm (US10$\frac{1}{2}$) needles.

Beg with a K row, cont in st st, inc 1 st at each end of next and every foll 5th[5th:5th:5th:5th:6th] row until there are 44[50:58:66:70:74] sts.

Cont without further shaping until work measures 30[36:42:46: 48:49]cm, 11$\frac{3}{4}$[14$\frac{1}{4}$:16$\frac{1}{2}$:18$\frac{1}{4}$:19:19$\frac{1}{4}$]ins from beg, ending with a WS row.

Shape top

Dec 1st at each end of every row until 32[38:44:52:54:58] sts rem.

Cast off loosely.

TO MAKE UP / TO FINISH

Join right shoulder seam.

NECKBAND

Using $4\frac{1}{2}$mm (US7) needles, with RS of work facing, K up 14[14:16:16: 18:18] sts down left side of neck, K across 8[10:10:14:18:20] sts at centre front, K up 14[14:16:16:18:18] sts up right side of neck, then K across 16[22:22:26:30:32] sts on back neck. 52[60:64:72:84:88] sts. Cont in K1, P1 rib for 2[2:2:5:2.5:3:3]cm, $\frac{3}{4}$ [$\frac{3}{4}$:1:1:1$\frac{1}{4}$:1$\frac{1}{4}$]ins.

Cast off loosely in rib.

Join left shoulder and neckband seam. Set in sleeves. Join side and sleeve seams.

A bowl of sweetly scented pot-pourri provides a delightful welcome to a room or can prove an original present with a personal touch. Its contents can be gathered from the garden or from the surrounding countryside.

POT-POURRI

A pot-pourri is a sweet-smelling medley of dried flowers, petals, leaves, citrus fruit peel and seeds to which have been added spices and essential oils. A fixative, such as common or sea salt, powdered orris root, gum benzoin or storax, is also needed to prevent the essential oils, and consequently the pot-pourri, from losing its fragrance when exposed to the air.

Do not slavishly follow a recipe for a pot-pourri but experiment with different ingredients until you alight upon the fragrance that best suits your personal preferences. It is fun to create a different fragrance for each season of the year. A winter mix can include the spicy scents of cinnamon or juniper and contain dried berries, fir cones, citrus peel studded with cloves, star anise, lichen or scented bark and wood shavings. While one composed of lavender, rose petals, pinks and scented geranium leaves conjures up the fresh sweetness of a summer garden.

For a dry pot-pourri gather the fresh ingredients when they are at their best and most fragrant. The dew should have evaporated, the day be warm and the flowers not damaged in any way. Leaves should be picked when they are young and before the plant has come into flower. Their scent is then at its strongest. Spread them out to dry on muslin, net or paper stretched over boxes or frames that allow the air to circulate freely and then cover with a sheet of foil or muslin. To preserve the colour of the ingredients dry the mixture slowly in the shade; the petals or whole flower heads should be turned every few days until they are papery. Do not be tempted to use flowers past their best or in full bloom, as their petals will have lost their scent and be apt to curl and brown at the edges. The most successful pot-pourris contain one part dried aromatic leaves to seven parts scented flower petals, but today there are no precise rules and all sorts of scented plant material can be used to good effect. ■

BASIC RECIPE FOR DRY POT-POURRI

To every pint (600ml/2½ cups) of mixed dried flowers and leaves add 1tsp of mixed powdered spices (though spices such as pieces of cinnamon stick, star anise, juniper berries, etc, can be added in a non-powdered form), 1tbs of powdered orris root, which will act as a fixative, and a few drops of essential oil, no more than two kinds ever being used together. ■

Pot-pourri, herbal pillow and linen and wardrobe sachets

The idol temples of that race should by no means be destroyed, but only the idols in them. Take holy water and sprinkle it in these shrines, build altars and place relics in them. For if the shrines are well built, it is essential they should be changed from the worship of the devils to the service of the true God. When this people see that their shrines are not destroyed they will be able to banish error from their hearts and be more ready to come to the place they are familiar with, but now recognizing and worshipping the true God.

ST AUGUSTINE
(NOTED BY THE VENERABLE BEDE IN 597)

CHRISTMAS TRADITIONS

The seeds of Christmas were sown long before the arrival of Christ on earth, its timing and a number of its now much-loved traditions having originated with our pagan ancestors.

The Roman festival of Saturnalia fell on 17 December and lasted for several days. A time of anarchy and merrymaking in praise of the god Saturn, this was marked by a general amnesty and holiday. Unrestrained revelry ensued and masters would exchange places with their slaves, going so far as to wash their feet, a practice later taken up by devout Christians. Servants were also at liberty, without fear of retribution, to tell their employers what they thought of them. It is hoped that the employers had short memories.

Like us, the Romans obviously felt the need to break the long winter season with a celebration, a farewell to the deadness of winter and welcome to the rebirth of spring, light and warmth – as did the pagan Norsemen. Edith mentions the winter solstice which also falls at this time and, called Yule, was celebrated by this fierce tribe.

The early Christians skilfully refashioned these pagan celebrations to suit their own needs. Over the centuries the pagan beginnings of Christmas were forgotten and new traditions added. Christmas has been enjoyed ever since, except for a short period in this country, when it was suspended during the Commonwealth years. The Puritans considered it a vile, 'Popish' festival and banned its celebration, it only being restored under Charles II when the monarchy was reinstated.

By Edith's day, Christmas was once again in full swing, thanks to the Victorians who had injected it with a new vitality.

THE FIRST CRIB

The nativity scene, The Adoration, *was painted by the Pre-Raphaelite artist Edward Burne-Jones.*

Now three years before his death it befell that he was minded, at the town of Greccio, to celebrate the memory of the Birth of the Child Jesus, with all the added solemnity that he might, for the kindling of devotion. That this might not seem an innovation, he sought and obtained licence from the Supreme Pontiff, and then made ready a manger, and bade hay, together with an ox and an ass, be brought unto the place. The Brethren were called together, the folk assembled, the wood echoed with their voices, and that august night was made radiant and solemn with many bright lights, and with tuneful and sonorous praises. The man of God, filled with tender love, stood before the manger, bathed in tears, and overflowing with joy. Solemn Masses were celebrated over the manger, Francis, the Levite of Christ, chanting the Holy Gospel. Then he preached unto the folk standing round the Birth of the King in poverty, calling Him, when he wished to name Him, the Child of Bethlehem, by reason of his tender love for Him. A certain knight, valorous and true, Messer John of Greccio, who for the love of Christ had left the secular army, and was bound by closest friendship unto the man of God, declared that he beheld a little Child right fair to see sleeping in that manger, Who seemed to be awakened from sleep when the blessed Father Francis embraced him in both arms. This vision of the knight is rendered worthy of belief, not alone through the holiness of him that beheld it, but is also confirmed by the truth that it set forth, and withal proven by the miracles that followed it. For the ensample of Francis, if meditated upon by the world, must needs stir up sluggish hearts unto the faith of Christ, and the hay that was kept back from the manger by the folk proved a marvellous remedy for sick beasts, and a prophylactic against divers other plagues, God magnifying by all means His servant, and making manifest by clear and miraculous portents the efficacy of his holy prayers.

ST BONAVENTURE, *LIFE OF ST FRANCIS OF ASSISI*

from CHRISTMAS

The bells of waiting Advent ring,
The Tortoise stove is lit again
And Lamp-oil light across the night
Has caught the streaks of winter rain
In many a stained-glass window sheen
From Crimson Lake to Hooker's Green.

The holly in the windy hedge
And round the Manor House the yew
Will soon be stripped to deck the ledge,
The altar, font and arch and pew
So that the villagers can say
The church looks nice' on Christmas
Day . . .

And is it true? And is it true,
This most tremendous tale of all,
Seen in a stained-glass window's hue,
A Baby in an ox's stall?
The Maker of the stars and sea
Become a Child on earth for me?

And is it true? For if it is,
No loving fingers tying strings
Around those tissued fripperies,
The sweet and silly Christmas things,
Bath salts and inexpensive scent
And hideous tie so kindly meant,

No love that in a family dwells,
No carolling in frosty air,
Nor all the steeple-shaking bells
Can with this single Truth compare -
That God was Man in Palestine
And lives to-day in Bread and Wine.
                    JOHN BETJEMAN

The gentle charm of the nativity has always held its appeal, whether celebrated in Greccio in 1224 or, centuries later, in suburbs like Crimson Lake or Hooker's Green.

DECEMBER

December was the last month of the old Roman year which was divided into ten months.

The Saxons called it 'winter-monat' or winter month, and 'heligh-monat', or holy month, from the fact that Christmas fell within it. The 22nd of December is the date of the winter solstice, when the sun reaches the tropic of Capricorn.

SAINT'S DAYS ETC.
Dec. 25. Christmas Day
Dec. 29. St Thomas' Day
Dec. 31. New Year's Eve.

The early Christian wished to celebrate the birth of Jesus, but having no facts to go by as to the day of his birth, settled on a variety of different dates, depending on which faction they belonged to. Happily, in 354 Pope Gregory proclaimed that 25 December was the correct date, for it fell nine months after 25 March, the celebration of the Annunciation of the Virgin. Cribs in churches and homes did not make an appearance until 1224, and St Francis of Assisi is to be thanked for introducing the tradition of recreating the nativity. Characteristically, he used a live ox and ass, and the scene of that first celebration of the nativity described here must have been a moving occasion.

MOTTOES
Bounce buckram velvets dear,
Christmas comes but once a year,
When it comes it brings good cheer,
And when it's gone, it's never near.

In December keep yourself warm
and sleep.

A green Yule, makes a fat kirk-yard.
                    COUNTRY DIARY

Anon, The Adoration of the Kings

Since the Holden family were enthusiastic readers of poetry, *On the Lincolnshire Coast* might well have been one of their Christmas favourites. Tennyson was certainly the foremost poet of his day, Poet Laureate indeed. Here he evokes the striking contrast between the bitter cold outside, and inside, goodwill and warmth.

ON THE LINCOLNSHIRE COAST

The time draws near the birth of Christ:
The moon is hid; the night is still;
The Christmas bells from hill to hill
Answer each other in the mist.

Four voices of four hamlets round,
From far and near, on mead and moor,
Swell out and fail, as if a door
Were shut between me and the sound:

Each voice four changes on the wind,
That now dilate, and now decrease,
Peace and goodwill, goodwill and peace
Peace and goodwill, to all mankind . . .

The time admits not flowers or leaves
To deck the banquet. Fiercely flies
The blast of North and East, and ice
Makes daggers at the sharpen'd eaves,

And bristles all the brakes and thorns
To yon hard crescent, as she hangs
Above the wood which grides and clangs
Its leafless ribs and iron horns

Together, in the drifts that pass
To darken on the rolling brine
That breaks the coast. But fetch the wine,
Arrange the board and brim the glass;

Bring in great logs and let them lie,
To make a solid core of heat;
Be cheerful-minded, talk and treat
Of all things ev'n as he were by.

We keep the day. With festal cheer,
With books and music, surely we
Will drink to him, whate'er he be,
And sing the songs he loved to hear.

ALFRED, LORD TENNYSON

The Society column of any newspaper has always been popular with its readership and the Edwardians were fascinated by the life of the royal family. Edward VII had a zest for life and recaptured the affections of his people, who had been dismayed at Queen Victoria's reclusive and mournful lifestyle.

SOCIAL AND PERSONAL

Their Majesties' Christmas The growing inclination to revive the old-fashioned Christmas within the present reign is strongly emphasised this year, when all the large country houses are crowded with guests.

Christmas trees for young and old, dances, theatricals, children's parties, hunting meats, breakfasts and balls, and entertainments for the servants and tenantry are all included in the programme for the observance of the festival.

The King and Queen have set the example, and the Sandringham party at this season is that of a typical English home.

Their Majesties have surrounded themselves with friends, and there is a giant Christmas tree laden with gifts for every member of the party, as well as toys and instructive games for the Royal grandchildren. Every article is chosen with due regard to the age and tastes of the recipient, and Queen Alexandra personally superintends the distribution.

At York Cottage The Prince and Princess of Wales left London on Saturday to join their children at York Cottage.

Prince Edward, with his brothers, and Princess Mary, look forward eagerly to the Christmas festival, and Santa Claus has as much interest for them as for children of humbler rank. A special Christmas tree is provided for the young princes, whose favourite toys are motorboats and trains, and other mechanical contrivances.

Charles Robinson, Christmas Morning

The old wooden rocking-horse so much in request a generation ago is as dead as the dodo, and is superseded by fat elephants which are 'warranted safe and quiet to ride', and are the popular mounts of the two youngest princes.

December has been an exciting month for the Prince of Wales's children, all of whom have been busy contriving presents for their parents and grandparents. Great secrecy prevails in the Royal nursery as to the precise nature of the work in hand. Princess Mary is, as usual, the leader of these small conspiracies to provide surprise gifts.

The little princess is expert with the knitting and crochet needles. She turns out a regular stock of well-made silk ties for her father and her uncles, as well as motor scarves, one of which the King received as a birthday gift. ■

***DAILY CHRONICLE,* 25 DECEMBER 1905**

A DICKENSIAN CHRISTMAS

Christmas time! That man must be a misanthrope indeed, in whose breast something like a jovial feeling is not roused – in whose mind some pleasant associations are not awakened – by the recurrence of Christmas. There are people who will tell you that Christmas is not to them what it used to be; that each succeeding Christmas has found some cherished hope, or happy prospect, of the year before, dimmed or passed away; that the present only serves to remind them of reduced circumstances and straitened incomes – of the feasts they once bestowed on hollow friends, and of the cold looks that meet them now, in adversity and misfortune. Never heed such dismal reminiscences. There are few men who have lived long enough in the world, who cannot call up such thoughts any day in the year. Then do not select the merriest of the three hundred and sixty-five for your doleful recollections, but draw your chair nearer the blazing fire – fill the glass and send round the song – and if your room be smaller than it was a dozen years ago, or if your glass be filled with reeking punch, instead of sparkling wine, put a good face on the matter, and empty it off-hand, and fill another, and troll off the old ditty you used to sing, and thank God it's no worse . . .

Who can be insensible to the outpourings of good feeling, and the honest interchange of affectionate attachment which abound at this season of the year. A Christmas family-party! We know nothing in nature more delightful! There seems a magic in the very name of Christmas. Petty jealousies and discords are forgotten; social feelings are awakened, in bosoms to which they have long been strangers; father and son, or brother and sister, who have met and passed with averted gaze, or a look of cold recognition, for months before, proffer and return the cordial embrace, and bury their past animosities in their present happiness. Kindly hearts that have yearned towards each other but have been withheld by false notions of pride and self-dignity, are again reunited, and all is kindness and benevolence! Would that Christmas lasted the whole year through (as it ought) and that the prejudices and passions which deform our better nature were never called into action among those to whom they should ever be strangers!

CHARLES DICKENS, *SKETCHES BY BOZ*

Charles Dickens, the most human and colourful of all Victorian storytellers, distils the essence of Christmas in this extract from *Sketches by Boz*. Above all, Christmas is a time of 'goodwill to all men' and family conviviality.

The following satirical look at Christmas pokes
fun at those who wished 'to get on in Society',
a major preoccupation of the times.

RE-INSTATING CHRISTMAS
BROADLANDS, YULETIDE

DEAREST DAPHNE, Didn't I *tell* you that, in my new position,
with unlimited cash at my back, I meant to bring off some big
things? I've begun already, though only two months married.
I've Re-instated Christmas, with my *Yuletide Revels* at *Broad-
lands*. Yes, my dear, thanks to your own BLANCHE, Christmas
will no longer be voted poky and middle-class. I got together a
lovely crowd, and we put in a simply ripping time...

We'd holly and mistletoe everywhere, a great yule log burning
in the hall, and all the traditional dishes at dinner, with snapdragon afterwards. Christmas Eve we all hung out our socks
and stockings, and went round putting the most absurd things
we could think of into them, though BOSH said nothing we
could *put in* would be so absurd as what had been *taken out* of
some of them.

I revived all the old Christmas customs I could think of. The
Vicaress here and some of the other local people helped me.
The Waits came, and sang carols and things, and we had them
in and gave them *wassail*...

I gave them all a *lovely* surprise on Christmas night. The
Mummers came round (they were the same village creatures as
the Waits; the Vicaress and I had drilled them, and I got their
dresses from town). They came into the hall and went on just
as the Mummers used to go on in the Middle Ages. NORTY said
they didn't *mum* properly and that one of them was tipsy, which
I think was distinctly horrid of him.

Then, when the *Mummers* were gone, we sat round the Yule
Log and roasted chestnuts and told stories – fact or fiction –
but they had to be original (as NORTY, who was at his very
wittiest, said, the chestnuts we were roasting were the only ones
allowed)...

NORTY was quite wonderful in finding out old Christmas
games for us to play. I'd no idea he was so learned or that
people all that time ago had such a good notion of amusing
themselves...

He constituted himself Lord of Misrule, and set us all playing
the most absurd old games. He said people used to play them
in the thirteenth and fourteenth centuries. JOSIAH turned
glumpy and said he didn't believe they were *ever* played, *then*

or at any other time, and Aunt GOLDIE backed him up. Poor
thing, she had tried desperately hard all day to be young and
keep pace with us, but she couldn't stay the distance, she was
short of gallops from the first, and at last crumpled up entirely
and vanished to the upper regions.

Everyone's been so sweet, loading me with congrats on my
success in getting Christmas out of the lumber-room. The
'Sideglancer,' the 'Peeress' and 'West-End Whispers' have all
written to ask for interviews and photos, and they want me
to send them articles on 'Christmas as an Opportunity for
Hostesses,' 'Christmas Redivivus,' and so on...

The King or Lord of Misrule, (LEFT) an ebullient character who traditionally led the Christmas revelries, had medieval beginnings. He was elected on 31 October to lead the revels through Christmas to Candlemas, 2 February. He and his officers would orchestrate the fun, ape ecclesiastical rituals and cause general mayhem. He was ultimately banned by the Puritans and never reinstated his seasonal reign of chaos, possibly proving more than most could take.

It seems a pity, just as I'm enjoying such a blaze of triumph, that JOSIAH and I should have had our first – no, not *quarrel*, I never quarrel, it's too much trouble – but he began to complain of certain Christmas customs, the mistletoe and all that, you know.

'Why,' I said, 'you ought to be *immensely* proud that your wife has brought back Christmas. And you ought to *reverence* all those old Yuletide customs. Don't you know that we get the mistletoe and all its privileges *direct* from the Druids?'

And he actually said the Druids might be *somethinged*, and that, if they set all that nonsense going, they ought to have been ashamed of themselves. And he went on to say, 'Such romping and flirting may be pardonable in boys and girls, but *men* ought to have more sense, and *married women* more reserve and dignity. And I tell you plainly, BLANCHE,' he wound up, 'that I *expect* those qualities in my wife.'

'*Reserve? Dignity?*' I cried. 'My *dear* man, where *do* you pick up these weird, old-world expressions? And, if you wanted those qualities in your wife, why on *earth* didn't you look for her in the Middle Classes?' He said no more, and neither can I just now, except that I'm Ever thine, BLANCHE. ∎

PUNCH, 2 JANUARY 1907

The burning of yule logs or clogs dates from the days of the pagan Norsemen celebrating the winter solstice. The flames lapping around the log symbolized the warmth and colour of the return of spring. It was yet another pagan tradition adopted by good Christians, such as Washington Irving's squire.

Christmas Greetings.
Old times, Old friendships.

Anon, Bringing Home the Yule Log (*card*)

The grate had been removed from the wide overwhelming fireplace, to make way for a fire of wood, in the midst of which was an enormous log glowing and blazing, and sending forth a vast volume of light and heat; this I understood was the yule clog, which the squire was particular in having brought in and illumined on Christmas Eve, according to ancient custom.

The yule clog is a great log of wood, sometimes the root of a tree, brought into the house with great ceremony, on Christmas Eve, laid in the fireplace, and lighted with the brand of last year's clog. While it lasted, there was great drinking, singing, and telling of tales. Sometimes it is accompanied by Christmas candles; but in the cottages the only light was from the ruddy blaze of the great wood fire. The yule clog was to burn all night; if it went out, it was considered a sign of ill luck... The brand remaining from the yule clog is carefully put away to light the next year's Christmas fire.

WASHINGTON IRVING, *SKETCH BOOK*

WASSAIL CUP

2 3in/7.5cm cinnamon sticks

4 cloves

3 blades mace

1 ginger root

1 level teaspoon nutmeg

4 apples

4oz/125g/$\frac{1}{2}$ cup sugar

$\frac{1}{2}$ pint/300ml/1$\frac{1}{4}$ cups brown ale

$\frac{1}{2}$ pint/300ml/1$\frac{1}{4}$ cups cider

Core apples and sprinkle with sugar and water. Bake at 375°F/190°C or gas no. 5 for 30 minutes or until tender. Mix ale, cider and spices together. Heat but do not boil. Leave for 30 minutes. Strain and pour over roasted apples. Serve in a punch bowl.

NICHOLAS CULPEPER, *HERBAL*

Susan B. Pearse, Father Christmas at a Children's Party

Wassail, which originated in the Middle Ages, was a drink of hot ale, apples, sugar and spices, also known as 'Lamb's Wool' because of the floating pulped apples. Served in a wooden bowl decorated with ribbons and evergreens, it would be handed around the company or carried from house to house. The word 'wassail', from the Anglo-Saxon for 'be whole', was a greeting equivalent to our 'good health', to be exchanged and offered to the season.

For us, today, Christmas would be barren indeed without the figure of Santa Claus or Father Christmas. But the bucolic white-haired old man dressed in red, his sleigh drawn by reindeer – such a familiar figure to Edwardian children – was, in fact, a recent nineteenth-century innovation from America. His roots run deep though, back to the Europe of centuries ago. His ancestor was St Nicholas, who was born in Asia Minor in the fourth century. The patron saint of boys and girls, he traditionally rode on a grey horse; and there is a legend that he saved three girls from prostitution by throwing bags of gold, a dowry, in to their window. On his feast day on 6 December, children in Europe, especially Holland, celebrate by exchanging gifts or writing to Santa Claus (*Sinte Klaas*) with their Christmas requests.

Dutch School, St Nicholas

The *Daily Chronicle* describes a happy mix of seasonal charity and magic proffered by the Carlton Hotel – who doubtless did quite well out of the teas partaken, as well as the publicity.

To step out of the mud and mire of Pall Mall yesterday evening into the Carlton Hotel was to pass into a brilliant glittering fairyland – for in the palm court of the hotel a giant Christmas tree stood, its branches burdened with toys and crackers and shimmering with tinsel and coloured electric lights. Underfoot was an imitation snow carpet spread with Jack Frost, while all around one were winter scenery and Christmas accessories.

It was certainly a good idea of the Carlton Hotel management to help the poor in this way, for juvenile visitors whose parents or uncles took them to tea at the Carlton yesterday were given some really splendid toys – there were over 600 of them – and were at the same time asked to drop something in one of

*Here comes I, Father Christmas
    am I,
Welcome – or welcome not;
I hope olde Father Christmas
Will never be forgot . . .
. . . Christmas comes but once
    a year
When it comes it brings good
    cheer;
With a pocket full of money
And a cellar full of beer,
Roast beef, plum pudding and
    mince pie,
Who likes them better than I?*
                    FROM AN ANCIENT
                    MUMMER'S PLAY

the money boxes that were fixed about the court. The money thus collected was sent last night to the children in hospital and charitable institutions, while the surplus toys were also forwarded, while the tree will stand for a few more days and then will be given up for the delight of the Lord Mayor's crippled children. ■
DAILY CHRONICLE, 25 DECEMBER 1906

Father Christmas is constantly being updated and here, in this Christmas card entitled A Merry Christmas (Anon), *we see him receiving requests from children by telephone. By 1902 London could boast of seven exchanges, though it is doubtful if children were allowed to use the telephone so freely, if at all. When first introduced, the telephone was not considered a vehicle for a good gossip, as it is today, but used purely for making arrangements or placing orders.*

The exchanging of presents at this time of year was introduced to England from Germany around 1840 and rapidly became the high point of Christmas for the Edwardian child. Who, like Ernest Shepard, has not woken when it was still dark on Christmas morning and crawled to the end of the bed in high excitement to explore the contents of a bulging stocking?

As we were going to sit up for late dinner on Christmas night, we were packed off to bed early. I did not mind this, as it was good to lie in bed and contemplate the morrow. I could hear the sound of church bells and the distant shoutings of the poulterer as he sold off his turkeys. Cyril and I had hung our stockings at the foot of the bed, and I tried to keep awake to see what happened in the night, but my effort was of no avail.

Waking up on Christmas morning in childhood is something that can never be forgotten. First I was conscious of something different about the day, then I remembered, and crawled to the bottom of the bed. It was all right! The stocking was full! I fumbled in the dark and turned out one thing after another. Some were done up in paper. There were crackers and an orange, and an exciting hard box which promised chocolates. I called to Cyril and found he too was exploring in the dark. Then he boldly got out of bed and lit the gas, standing on a chair. This was not allowed, but we felt that on Christmas morning it was different. We laid all our gifts on the bed and opened the chocolates.

Presently we heard the sound of movement downstairs, and Martha came in. We shouted 'Happy Christmas' but she was shocked at the gas, and said, 'You know what your Father told you!' We tried to pacify her with chocolates, but the only result was for her to tell us to put them away, else we'd make ourselves sick. We got into our dressing-gowns and

Viggo Johansen, Happy Christmas

went down to Ethel's room. She was sitting up in bed and feeling as excited over her stocking as we were over ours.

Then we remembered about singing, and went and stood outside Mother's room and sang her a Christmas carol. She came to the door and we all hugged

her and wished her a happy Christmas. After we were dressed, Cyril and I hurried downstairs to arrange our cards and little gifts on Mother's and Father's plates, and to gaze in anticipation at the sideboard piled high with parcels. Then we went to the kitchen to greet Lizzie

Not everyone, of course, receives the gift of their dreams but it is to be hoped that the recipient appreciates, more than Reginald, the spirit in which it was given.

Karl Rogers, Father Christmas

and to tie a ribbon on Sambo; we did not stay long, for Lizzie was already busy making preparations for Christmas Dinner. ∎

ERNEST H. SHEPARD,
DRAWN FROM MEMORY

REGINALD ON CHRISTMAS PRESENTS

I wish it to be distinctly understood (said Reginald) that I don't want a 'George, Prince of Wales' Prayer-book as a Christmas present. The fact cannot be too widely known.

There ought (he continued) to be technical education classes on the science of present-giving. No one seems to have the faintest notion of what any one else wants, and the prevalent ideas on the subject are not creditable to a civilized community.

There is, for instance, the female relative in the country who 'knows a tie is always useful,' and sends you some spotted horror that you could only wear in secret or in Tottenham Court Road. It *might* have been useful had she kept it to tie up currant bushes with, when it would have served the double purpose of supporting the branches and frightening away the birds – for it is an admitted fact that the ordinary tomtit of commerce has a sounder aesthetic taste than the average female relative in the country.

Then there are aunts. They are always a difficult class to deal with in the matter of presents. The trouble is that one never catches them really young enough. By the time one has educated them to an appreciation of the fact that one does not wear red woollen mittens in the West End, they die, or quarrel with the family, or do something equally inconsiderate. That is why the supply of trained aunts is always so precarious.

There is my Aunt Agatha, *par exemple,* who sent me a pair of gloves last Christmas, and even got so far as to choose a kind that was being worn and had the correct number of buttons. But – *they were nines!* I sent them to a boy whom I hated intimately: he didn't wear them, of course, but he could have – that was where the bitterness of death came in. It was nearly as consoling as sending white flowers to his funeral. Of course I wrote and told my aunt that they were the one thing that had been wanting to make existence blossom like a rose; I am afraid she thought me frivolous – she comes from the North, where they live in the fear of Heaven and the Earl of Durham.

Even friends of one's own set, who might be expected to

know better, have curious delusions on the subject. I am *not* collecting copies of the cheaper editions of Omar Khayyam. I gave the last four that I received to the lift-boy, and I like to think of him reading them, with FitzGerald's notes, to his aged mother. Lift-boys always have aged mothers; shows such nice feeling on their part, I think.

Anon, Toys for Christmas (*card*)

Personally, I can't see where the difficulty in choosing suitable presents lies. No boy who had brought himself up properly could fail to appreciate one of those decorative bottles of liqueurs that are so reverently staged in Morel's window – and it wouldn't in the least matter if one did get duplicates. And there would always be the supreme moment of dreadful uncertainty whether it was *crême de menthe* or Chartreuse – like the expectant thrill on seeing your partner's hand turned up at bridge. People may say what they like about the decay of Christianity; the religious system that produced green Chartreuse can never really die.

And then, of course, there are liqueur glasses, and crystallized fruits, and tapestry curtains and heaps of other necessaries of life that make really sensible presents – not to speak of luxuries, such as having one's bills paid, or getting something quite sweet in the way of jewellery. Unlike the alleged Good Woman of the Bible, I'm not above rubies. When found, by the way, she must have been rather a problem at Christmas-time; nothing short of a blank cheque would have fitted the situation. Perhaps it's as well that she's died out.

The great charm about me (concluded Reginald) is that I am so easily pleased. But I draw the line at a 'Prince of Wales' prayer-book.

SAKI (H.H. MUNRO), *WESTMINSTER GAZETTE*

CHRISTMAS CARDS

Christmas cards were first introduced in 1846 by Henry Cole, the first Director of the Victoria and Albert Museum, and before long they became an accepted part of the build-up to the big day. So meteoric was their rise in popularity that by the end of the century the Postmaster General was urging the public to 'Post Early for Christmas'. Although snow scenes, robins, holly and coachloads of merrymakers were popular, there seemed no rules to follow when it came to subject-matter, however unseasonal. Humorous cards abounded but those of a religious nature were rare.

Posting the Christmas Cards.

With all our best wishes for the Season.

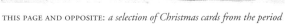

THIS PAGE AND OPPOSITE: *a selection of Christmas cards from the period*

Mr Pooter in George and Weedon Grossmith's
The Diary of a Nobody was loath to be found wanting
in minor social courtesies and surprisingly extravagant
when it came to buying Christmas cards.

THE DIARY OF A NOBODY

December 20 Went to Smirksons', the drapers, in the Strand,
who this year have turned out everything in the shop and
devoted the whole place to the sale of Christmas cards. Shop
crowded with people, who seemed to take up the cards rather
roughly, and, after a hurried glance at them, throw them down
again. I remarked to one of the young persons serving, that
carelessness appeared to be a disease with some pur-
chasers. The observation was scarcely out of my
mouth, when my thick coat-sleeve caught against a
large pile of expensive cards in boxes one on top of
the other, and threw them down. The manager came
forward, looking very much annoyed, and picking
up several cards from the ground, said to one of the
assistants, with a palpable side-glance at me: 'Put
these amongst the sixpenny goods; they can't be sold
for a shilling now.' The result was, I felt it my duty
to buy some of these damaged cards.

I had to buy more and pay more than intended.
Unfortunately I did not examine them all, and when
I got home I discovered a vulgar card with a picture
of a fat nurse with two babies, one black and the
other white, and the words: 'We wish Pa a Merry
Christmas.' I tore up the card and threw it away.
Carrie said the great disadvantage of going out in
Society and increasing the number of our friends
was, that we should have to send out nearly two
dozen cards this year. ∎

December 21 To save the postman a miserable
Christmas, we follow the example of all unselfish
people, and send out our cards early. Most of the
cards had fingermarks, which I did not notice at
night. I shall buy all future cards in the daytime.
Lupin (who, ever since he has had the appointment
with a stock and share broker, does not seem over-
scrupulous in his dealings) told me never to rub out
the pencilled price on the backs of the cards. I asked
him why. Lupin said: 'Suppose your card is marked
9d. Well, all you have to do is to pencil a 3 – and a
long down-stroke after it – in *front* of the ninepence,
and people will think you have given five times the
price for it.' ∎

Karl Rogers, Father Christmas with Children

GOD REST YOU MERRY GENTLEMEN

God rest you merry, gentlemen,
Let nothing you dismay,
For Jesus Christ our Saviour
Was born upon this day,
To save us all from Satan's power
When we were gone astray:
O tidings of comfort and joy.

In Bethlehem in Jewry
This blessèd babe was born,
And laid within a manger
Upon this blessed morn;
The which his mother Mary
Nothing did take in scorn:

From God our heavenly Father
A blessèd angel came,
And unto certain shepherds
Brought tidings of the same,
How that in Bethlehem was born
The Son of God by name:

'Fear not,' then said the angel,
'Let nothing you afright,
This day is born a Saviour
Of virtue, power, and might;
So frequently to vanquish all
The friends of Satan quite:'

The Shepherds at those tidings
Rejoicèd much in mind,
And left their flocks a-feeding
In tempest, storm and wind,
And went to Bethlehem straightway
This blessèd babe to find:

But when to Bethlehem they came,
Whereat this infant lay,
They found him in a manger
Where oxen feed on hay,
His mother Mary kneeling
Unto the Lord did pray:

Now to the Lord sing praises,
All you within this place,
And with true love and brotherhood
Each other now embrace;
This holy tide of Christmas
All others doth deface:
TRADITIONAL

The words and music of 'God Rest You Merry Gentlemen' are traditional and were collected by William Sandys, one of a band of Victorian antiquaries who rediscovered our precious heritage.

Anon, Carol Singers (*postcard*)

The old French *carole*, both a spirited and often robust song and ring dance, was adopted by the English in about 1300. But it was not long before the church stepped in and altered the words and significance of these lively songs. By the sixteenth century they became exclusive to Christmas but, banned during the Commonwealth years, later died out in this country. It was only thanks to the enthusiasm of Victorian folklorists that this essential ingredient of Christmas was reinstated and given new vigour.

The custom of singing from house to house began in Victorian times. Happily, Hardy's band of singers and musicians were well rewarded by the sight of the school teacher appearing at her window to thank them: as one of them commented afterwards, 'As near a thing to a spiritual vision as ever *I* wish to see.'

Percy Tarrant, The Entertainer

THE MELLSTOCK ROUNDS

By this time they were crossing to a wicket in the direction of the school, which, standing on a slight eminence on the opposite side of a cross lane, now rose in unvarying and dark flatness against the sky. The instruments were re-tuned, and all the band entered the enclosure, enjoined by old William to keep upon the grass.

'Number seventy-eight,' he softly gave out as they formed round in a semicircle, the boys opening the lanterns to get a clearer light, and directing their rays on the books. Then passed forth into the quiet night an ancient and well-worn hymn, embodying Christianity in words peculiarly befitting the simple and honest hearts of the quaint characters who sang them so earnestly.

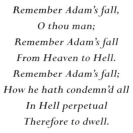

Remember Adam's fall,
O thou man;
Remember Adam's fall
From Heaven to Hell.
Remember Adam's fall;
How he hath condemn'd all
In Hell perpetual
Therefore to dwell.

Remember God's goodness,
O thou man:
Remember God's goodness,
His promise made.
Remember God's goodness
He sent His Son sinless
Our ails for to redress,
Our hearts to aid.

In Bethlehem He was born,
O thou man:
In Bethlehem He was born,

For mankind's sake.
In Bethlehem He was born,
Christmas Day i' the morn;
Our Saviour did not scorn
Our faults to take.

Give thanks to God alway,
O thou man:
Give thanks to God alway
With heart-felt joy.
Give thanks to God alway
On this our joyful day:
Let all men sing and say,
Holy, Holy!

WITH CAROL SWEET AND MERRY LAY
WE GLADLY WELCOME NEW YEAR'S DAY!

Anon, Carol Singers (*card*)

Having concluded the last note, they listened for a minute or two, but found that no sound issued from the school-house.

'Forty breaths, and then "O, what unbounded goodness!" number fifty-nine,' said William.

This was duly gone through, and no notice whatever seemed to be taken of the performance.

'Surely 'tisn't an empty house, as befell us in the year thirty-nine and forty-three!' said old Dewy with much disappointment.

'Perhaps she's jist come from some noble city, and sneers at our doings,' the tranter whispered.

' 'Od rabbit her!' said Mr Penny, with an annihilating look at a corner of the school chimney. 'I don't quite stomach her, if this is it. Your plain music well done is as worthy as your other sort done bad, 'a b'lieve, souls; so say I.'

'Forty breaths, and then the last,' said the leader authoritatively. ' "Rejoice, ye tenants of the earth," number sixty-four.'

At the close, waiting yet another minute. he said in a clear loud voice, as he had said in the village at that hour and season for the previous forty years:

'A merry Christmas to ye!' ■

THOMAS HARDY, *UNDER THE GREENWOOD TREE*

Not all carol singers would be satisfied with so little and some might need some expert instruction on how to achieve financial rather than spiritual reward.

THE CAROL ACADEMY

The Daily Express of December 20 states that is has discovered a school for the training of young carol-cadgers, presided over by an expert ex-beggar and especially flourishing about Christmas time. We are fortunate in obtaining a rough-drafted prospectus of the same. The subjects of instruction include:

Variations on three well-known Hymn-tunes, or, How to sing in several keys at once.
The Art of Repetition, or Boring for Coppers.
Carolling into Keyholes, with Hints on being kick-proof.
Some Useful Repartees, on being sent empty away.
Lugubriousness as an Aid to Moneymaking.
The Borrowed Baby, and where to Pinch it within earshot of the Philanthropic.
How to avoid being Pinched (by the Police).
The Whole Theory of being a Public Nuisance.

Professor Fagin receives pupils of any age from three years upwards, exhibitions being granted to infants in arms. The third and fourth cadgers of a family pay half-fees, which in ordinary cases are the price of a pot of beer per hymn-tune, and 50 per cent extra with words. All fees are strictly payable in advance. Applications for admission to the Academy may be made at any time to the Principal by Parents or Guardians, there being no irksome restrictions as to Health Certificates or Character. The sole qualification is the possession of a pair of lungs. ■

PUNCH, JANUARY 1907

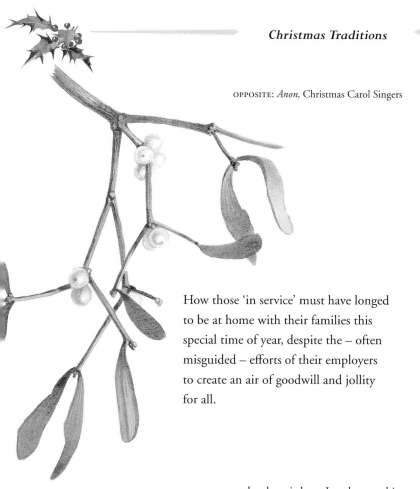

OPPOSITE: *Anon,* Christmas Carol Singers

How those 'in service' must have longed to be at home with their families this special time of year, despite the – often misguided – efforts of their employers to create an air of goodwill and jollity for all.

THE TREE

I have not written much lately. We have all been busy getting ready for Christmas, buying presents for people, and keeping the secret, and wondering who's going to send us presents and what they'll be like, and doing up the house in holly and mistletoe. We hung a bit of mistletoe to the chandelier in the hall, and I went to Mrs AUSTIN and told her somebody wanted to see her – somebody she knew very well, but I wasn't to mention his name. She said she must make herself tidy, but I told her he couldn't wait more than half a minute and she must come at once. So she came, and when I got her

under the mistletoe I took a good jump at her and gave her a kiss, a regular smacker. She couldn't make it out, but I told her to look up, and then she knew. She said she never did see such a owdacious young spark in all her born days, but she didn't mind really... NINA said if JIM tried to kiss her she would plunge a stiletto in his something heart. I think the word was recarrent, or something like that. I hadn't heard it before, and when I asked NINA she said she wasn't quite sure how it was spelt. She said she had once heard it in a theatre. The man who had that heart, she said, was a villain.

But the best joke we had was the Christmas-tree for everybody – for us and the servants and all. It was to be at half-past four, and we were all to have tea together in the dining-room afterwards.

The tree was in the school-room upstairs. We'd covered it all over with presents, and there were a lot more laid on the floor under it and on the earth round about. It was in a box. There were candles all the way up it, and strings of silvery balls, and all the things they put on Christmas trees. NINA was the Spirit of the Season. She was a real fairy this time, and no mistake. She had a muslin dress and a pair of wings, and a wand done up in silver paper. First the servants all came in... Mum was there, too, and Uncle DICK and Aunt Margery. They were spending Christmas with us. All the servants sat round the wall on chairs and never said a word. They were all dressed in their Sunday best and looked very uncomfortable...

Well, they all sat there as glum as possible, and every now and then Mum said a word to one of them and they whispered something back. Mrs AUSTIN was in black silk, and she looked hotter than ever. First NINA came in and she danced round the room, and then she stopped in front of the tree and said a bit of poetry. She said it was a glad season and everybody was joyful. Happiness was spread all over the earth, and the people in it were having heaps of mirth. She said she could hear the sounds of rejoicing and laughter, and she told them now was the time to throw care away and join in revelry on this festal day. It was something like that, and she did it very well, but they all sat there quite silent till Uncle DICK said, 'Bravo, little 'un,' and then they began to clap their hands and whisper to one another. Then NINA went and sat on Mum's lap, and there was a loud knock at the door. I knew who it was and dashed to open it, and in came Santa Claus – Dad, of course, but I didn't tell the rest...

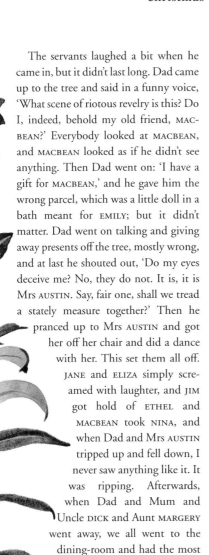

The servants laughed a bit when he came in, but it didn't last long. Dad came up to the tree and said in a funny voice, 'What scene of riotous revelry is this? Do I, indeed, behold my old friend, MAC-BEAN?' Everybody looked at MACBEAN, and MACBEAN looked as if he didn't see anything. Then Dad went on: 'I have a gift for MACBEAN,' and he gave him the wrong parcel, which was a little doll in a bath meant for EMILY; but it didn't matter. Dad went on talking and giving away presents off the tree, mostly wrong, and at last he shouted out, 'Do my eyes deceive me? No, they do not. It is, it is Mrs AUSTIN. Say, fair one, shall we tread a stately measure together?' Then he pranced up to Mrs AUSTIN and got her off her chair and did a dance with her. This set them all off. JANE and ELIZA simply screamed with laughter, and JIM got hold of ETHEL and MACBEAN took NINA, and when Dad and Mrs AUSTIN tripped up and fell down, I never saw anything like it. It was ripping. Afterwards, when Dad and Mum and Uncle DICK and Aunt MARGERY went away, we all went to the dining-room and had the most gorgeous tea, and they all talked away and kept laughing like mad. It was a very jolly evening. ■

R.C. LEHMANN, *PUNCH*

For the cottagers of Lark Rise, Christmas was a relatively simple and peaceful day.

LARK RISE TO CANDLEFORD

Christmas Day passed very quietly. The men had a holiday from work and the children from school and the churchgoers attended special Christmas services. Mothers who had young children would buy them an orange each and a handful of nuts; but, except at the end house and the inn, there was no hanging up of stockings, and those who had no kind elder sister or aunt in service to send them parcels got no Christmas presents.

Still, they did manage to make a little festival of it. Every year the farmer killed an ox for the purpose and gave each of his men a joint of beef, which duly appeared on the Christmas dinner-table together with plum pudding – not Christmas pudding, but suet duff with a good sprinkling of raisins. Ivy and other evergreens (it was not a holly country) were hung from the ceiling and over the pictures; a bottle of homemade wine was uncorked, a good fire was made up, and, with doors and windows closed against the keen, wintry weather, they all settled down by their own firesides for a kind of super-Sunday. There was little visiting of neighbours and there were no family reunions, for the girls in service could not be spared at that season, and the few boys who had gone out in the world were mostly serving abroad in the Army.

There were still bands of mummers in some of the larger villages, and village choirs went carol-singing about the countryside; but none of these came to the hamlet, for they knew the collection to be expected there would not make it worth their while. A few families, sitting by their own firesides, would sing carols and songs; that, and more and better food and a better fire than usual, made up their Christmas cheer.

FLORA THOMPSON, *LARK RISE TO CANDLEFORD*

QUEEN VICTORIA'S CHRISTMAS TREE, 1848

The Christmas tree in the engraving is that which is annually prepared by her Majesty's command for the Royal children . . . The tree employed for this festive purpose is a young fir of about eight feet high, and has six tiers of branches. On each tier, or branch, are arranged a dozen wax tapers. Pendant from the branches are elegant trays, baskets, *bonbonnières*, and other receptacles for sweetmeats of the most varied and expensive kind; and of all forms, colours and degrees of beauty. Fancy cakes, gilt gingerbread and eggs filled with sweetmeats, are also suspended by variously coloured ribbons from the branches. The tree, which stands upon a table covered with white damask, is supported at the root by piles of sweets of a larger kind, and by toys and dolls of all descriptions, suited to the youthful fancy, and to the several ages of the interesting scions of Royalty for whose gratification they are displayed.

The trees are constructed and arranged by Mr Mawdill, the Queen's confectioner. ■

THE ILLUSTRATED LONDON NEWS, 1848

The decorated tree is an indispensable part of Christmas and the most-loved of Victorian introductions. Although fir trees decorated with paper roses, sweets, candles and apples were introduced from Germany to Britain before Prince Albert's day, it is he who is credited with popularizing them. By the end of the century well over 30,000 were being sold a year and were decorated by excited families – not, as in this picture, by a Royal confectioner.

In Scotland New Year is celebrated in preference to Christmas, various rituals being enacted and families joining together to eat and drink traditional food such as 'Hogmanay' cheese and oat cakes and *het pint,* a drink of spiced ale and whisky. A time of seeing the old year out and the new in, it also involved spring cleaning and the paying off of all debts. At midnight the door is flung open to welcome in the New Year, bells are rung and a riotous noise made to frighten away any unwelcome spirits. After 'Auld Lang Syne' has been sung the tradition of first-footing begins. Ideally, a red-haired man should enter the house carrying a branch of twigs and some mistletoe. The former would be placed on the fire, the latter on the mantelpiece. Or the first-footer could bring bread, salt and coal, symbolizing life, friendship and warmth. The tradition is fraught with superstition, it being bad luck if the first-footer should be a woman, be blind in one eye or have splayed feet.

With snow making such gatherings impossible on New Year's Eve 1906, many Scottish families must have had to do without their red-haired first-footer.

New Year cards. BELOW: *Anon,* The Ivy Garlands

Dec. 31 1906.
Hogmonay. There is a rise in the temperature this morning, the wind has gone round to the South West, and there is every sign of an approaching thaw. The papers report more falls of snow, out-lying farms and villages in Yorkshire, East Lothian, and the Highlands are entirely isolated by the deep snow.

COUNTRY DIARY

GREETINGS CARDS

Homemade Christmas cards are especially appreciated. The following two suggestions, not having a strictly seasonal flavour, can be treasured and enjoyed throughout the year.

Greetings cards need not be large; small cards are, in fact, usually more practical to send, and you will find it easier to buy matching envelopes. Designs can be very simple: a few flowers made into a small posy or a pattern running around the card to serve as a border for a small central

picture are ideal for this type of card. You must use good quality paper that is strong and will stand up easily when it has been folded in half.

Cut the piece of card or good quality stiff paper to size, bearing in mind that it will be folded in half. If you are planning to make many

cards, it might be wise to work out a size then buy a pack of matching envelopes. When you have cut the paper to size, this is the best moment to make a border, since a mistake with an outline pen once the flowers are firmly stuck to the paper would be disastrous. Use the finest pen possible; if you do want a wider line, make sure that the pen is not 'fluffy' as this will cause the lines to blur.

Next work out your design and glue it to the card. Make sure all the little pieces are firmly stuck down, then wait a while for the glue to dry. Place a piece of paper over the card and leave it under a heavy book for about an hour. Remove the paper and book, then measure sufficient transparent film to fit exactly over the card. Most rolls of film are made on backing paper printed with squares to help with the measuring. Working from the top of the card, unpeel the first part of the prepared film and place it very carefully on your design. Press this part down, then holding the card, unpeel the film little by little, until the whole design is covered. You should always smooth it as you go to prevent air bubbles forming. Trim any excess film from the sides and place the card again under the paper and books to settle the film.

GREETINGS CARDS EMBROIDERED WITH BIRDS

MEASUREMENTS

Embroidery designs (approx):
Card 1–$6\frac{1}{4}$in × $4\frac{1}{2}$in (16cm × 11cm)
Card 2–4in × $4\frac{1}{2}$in (10cm × 11cm)

MATERIALS

8in (20cm) square Aida fabric with 14 threads to 1in (2.5cm) for each card
Coats Anchor Stranded Cotton:
For single bird card: 1 skein each of White; Black; 0387; 0920; 0921; 0392; 0341; 0399; 0400; 0397; 0391; 0398; 0847; 0401; 0340; 0337; 0339; 0338; 0393; 0392; 0380
For 4 birds card: 1 skein each of White; Black; 0387; 0847; 0401; 0168; 0928; 0852; 0887; 0292; 0167; 0170; 0397; 0339; 0399; 0398; 0400; 0341; 0338; 0380; 0340; 0337; 0393; 0921; 0920; 0158; 0922
Tapestry needle No 24
Self-adhesive cards by Framecraft.
 Double-sided adhesive tape.
 Fabric adhesive.

TO MAKE

1 Fold fabric lightly widthwise and lengthwise to mark centre lines. Work tacking stitches along centre lines.

2 Centre of chart is indicated by arrows which should coincide with tacking stitches.

3 Work embroidery following chart and key for 'Birds' design, working as far as possible out from centre. Chart shows embroidery designs for both greeting cards. Broken line separates one design from the other.

4 Use 2 strands of cotton throughout. Each square on chart represents one intersection of threads (1 warp and 1 weft) or one cross stitch.

5 Remove tacking threads.

6 Place oval frame of card over embroidered motif. Mark where oval edges fall.

7 Trim fabric to fit inside card. Hold taut in position with double-sided adhesive tape.

Designs: a) 40× 43 stitches

b) 60× 43 stitches

14 stitches to 1in (2.5 cm):

Special instructions

Outline:

bluebirds   0399

brown birds

wing   0401

head   0399

foot   0380

breast   0393

eyes   *black*

red area in eyes   0339

Backstitch:

highlights in eyes   *ecru*

8 Peel off top half of tape and press down onto front of card; smooth in place.

9 If necessary, add a smear of fabric adhesive round the inside edge of oval.

Key	
/	white
●	black
‖	0387
∧	0398
—	0400
+	0399
S	0397
→	0167
C	0168
<	0928
T	0158
←	0380
I	0170
>	0341
↑	0340
V	0391
\	0338
⊃	0337
○	0847
↓	0922
=	0921
I	0920
Z	0393
H	0392
×	0887
—	0852
•	0292
△	0401
∩	0339

Shade numbers refer to Coats Anchor Stranded Cotton.

Papier maché work and the making of sweetly scented sachets and pillows were a popular pastime of the Edwardian lady, along with decorating screens with scrapwork, painting silk fans and fashioning flowers out of paper or wax. Such industry provided her with a cache of gifts for birthday and, of course, Christmas presents.

DECORATING PAPIER MÂCHÉ

YOU WILL NEED
A quantity of newspaper
Wallpaper adhesive and a medium width brush
A pot of Vaseline
A wide-rimmed bowl, plate or dish
FOR THE DECORATION
Acrylic paint
Pressed plant materials
Rubber-based glue (in a plate or saucer)
Orange sticks
Scissors
Tweezers
Plastic sealant

A papier mâché plate and pot, both decorated with pressed flowers, then sealed and varnished.

First, find an interesting shaped open bowl or dish; a salad bowl is ideal. Tear or cut masses of newspapers into strips. Magazines are also useful but should be used only after a quantity of the newspaper has been applied first. Rub Vaseline over the inside of the bowl or plate, making sure that it is coated thinly all over, right up to the rim and slightly over it.

Wet the first strips of paper with a little water, and mould them to the bottom of the bowl, smoothing them down so that there are no air bubbles. Each strip should overlap the last, and they should be brought right up and over the rim (they can be trimmed afterwards). Place the next layer on top of the first, using the wallpaper paste made up according to the instructions on the packet. Put three layers on altogether, and leave to dry for at least twenty-four hours; sometimes it will be necessary to leave it longer. When dry, build up the next layers until there are at least twelve. If you do fewer, the result will be too flimsy. When all the layers have dried properly, edge the shape out of the mould and tidy the edges. The Vaseline should have prevented any of the paper sticking to the base of the mould. Make sure that there are no gaps, where the paper is not sufficiently well stuck down, then take

an acrylic paint, mix the colour you have chosen and paint the bowl.

When the paint is dry and you have created the colours and effects you wish, you can prepare the pressed plant materials to go in position. When you have worked out the design, glue the flowers to the surface using a little rubber-based glue. Make sure each piece is stuck down firmly. When the glue is dry, apply a sealant over the plants and let it dry. Then apply six coats of varnish on both the top and the underside of the bowl or dish, dusting the surfaces before each coat is applied.

A papier mâché vase can be made in the same way, except you cover the outside of the container with paper. When the stages are complete, cut down neatly through the paper and then glue the two halves together, using a very strong paper glue.

It is possible to create many textures. You could, for example, place a layer of fine muslin over the bowl and glue it to the surface before painting; or you could use different widths of different papers, cut into shapes and stuck down to form a pattern. ■

SCENTED SACHETS AND PILLOWS

Pillows and sachets filled with fragrant pot-pourri.

It is said that the fragrance of hops will send you into the most glorious sleep. The gentle fragrance of herbs and flowers near the bedside gives great comfort and a feeling of well-being. Sachets and pillows are easy to make, and you do not have to be an expert at needlework. I buy pretty pillow slips and fabric cases at antique shops and on market stalls, make a lining to go inside them and then fill them with the fragrance of my choice. Some perfumes are too overpowering to have permanently near you, so I always choose a delicate herbal scent or softly fragranced flowers to fill the bags. Herbs such as lemon balm, mint, rosemary and sweet marjoram are all great favourites, and they can be used on their own or mixed with other scents. Lavender is wonderful on its own, and its perfume will last for years. Below are some simple mixes to

try and when you tire of one, just remove the sachet and make another.

There are two types of sachets. The first type are seen in drawers and on shelves, while the second is used for fragrancing a pillow and is not visible. To make the first type, you will want to choose a pretty fabric. Antique shops and market stalls as well as traditional material stores often have beautiful remnants for sale. Avoid materials with huge designs, which will be lost on these small sachets. Instead, choose pretty little flower designs, small stripes, check or even completely plain fabrics. Natural materials – cottons, silks and satins – are the nicest, and if you choose lace, you will probably have to line the inside with a fine, plain fabric or the pot-pourri will fall through the holes.

A SACHET FOR DRAWERS OR SHELVES

YOU WILL NEED

A rectangular piece of fabric,
12 × 8in (30 × 20cm)
A needle and thread
Sewing scissors
12–18in (30–45cm) ribbon
Pot-pourri
An iron

Turn the fabric inside out and fold it in half. Sew neatly up both the open sides, then fold the top of the bag about one-third of the way down and iron it flat. Place a stitch on each side so that the fabric will not slip back out. Turn the bag the right way out and fill it about two-thirds full of the pot-pourri. Take the ribbon, wind it around twice, tie a tight knot and then make a bow. The sachet is now ready to use.

AN INTERIOR SACHET

YOU WILL NEED

Rectangular piece of plain fabric,
12 × 8in (30 × 20cm)
Sewing scissors
A needle and thread
Pot-pourri
An iron

Turn the fabric inside out and fold it in half. Sew neatly up both the open sides, then turn the top of the bag back about 1in (2.5cm) down and iron flat. Catch each side with a piece of thread and turn the bag the right way out. Fill the bag with the pot-pourri and sew the top neatly together. Before leaving it inside a pillowcase, remove the pillow and sew two corners of the bag to the pillow to prevent it slipping. Do not make tight knots or it will be difficult to remove later on. Replace the pillow in the slip, and the sachet will almost immediately begin to fragrance the pillow.

SLEEP PILLOW

This quantity will
be sufficient
to fill three sachets
1oz (30g) hops
1oz (30g) rosemary
1oz (30g) lemon verbena leaves
1 drop lemon verbena oil

MIXED HERB SACHET

This quantity will fill four sachets
1oz (30g) peppermint leaves
1oz (30g) rosemary
1oz (30g) thyme
1oz (30g) lemon verbena
1oz (30g) sweet woodruff
1oz (30g) camomile flowers
1 drop lemon balm oil

ROSE SACHET

This quantity will fill three sachets
4oz (125g) rose petals
1oz (30g) whole rose buds
½oz (15g) whole cloves
½oz (15g) orris-root powder
2 drops damask rose oil

LAVENDER SACHET

This quantity will be sufficient to
fill two sachets
3oz (90g) lavender florets
1oz (30g) peppermint leaves
2 drops lavender oil

There are many combinations of herbs and flowers that are delightful when mixed together, and, as each person will prefer a different type of fragrance, experiment with herbs and flowers from your garden to produce wonderful results. Remember not to add too many drops of oil as the effect will be overpowering. ■

The Yew (*Taxus baccata***) is generally dicius, the male and female flowers being borne on different trees. Its poisonous properties reside in the foliage, the fleshy part of the berries being quite harmless, though the seed is injurious. Yew trees live to a great age, some in this country being recorded as a thousand years of age. It is supposed to have been planted by the Druids in their sacred groves. In later days it was planted in the church-yards as a symbol of mourning; and some say to provide bows for the archers.**

COUNTRY DIARY

CHRISTMAS DECORATIONS

It is hard to imagine a home, however rich or poor, devoid of any decoration at this time of year. The adornment of the house and tree, with the fun of choosing what to use and where, always generates an air of excitement and expectation. It is one of the most enjoyable of all Christmas customs. Even the poor cottagers in Flora Thompson's *Lark Rise to Candleford*, although unable to buy presents, saw to it that the house was hung with holly and ivy. They were fortunate in being able to roam the countryside to find what they needed but the city-dweller has a harder time of it: he has either to dip into his pocket to buy a sprig of holly or to set to and make his own paper decorations. The wealthy, of course, can afford to go to great lengths to create a festive air, and in Edwardian times for several days before Christmas the children in the nursery would industriously make paper roses and gild walnuts for the tree, whilst those below stairs and in the garden gathered and fashioned garlands and wreaths.

Living in the country, the Holdens would most probably have sallied forth to find ivy, yew, holly, fir cones and other natural materials that could be made into traditional and original decorations. Doubtless, Edith and her sisters' artistic eyes and imaginations would have been easily spurred into creativity by the varied shapes and textures of foliage, nuts and bark.

The making of Christmas decorations follows an ancient custom with pagan beginnings. The tradition of bringing evergreens into the house was thought by the Romans to bring good luck and was as an important part of the festival of Saturnalia as it is of Christmas. The evergreens symbolized everlasting life and both the holly and the ivy had their own special significance.

THE HOLLY AND THE IVY

The holly and the ivy,
When they are both full grown,
Of all the trees that are in the wood,
The holly bears the crown:
The rising of the sun
And the running of the deer,
The playing of the merry organ,
Sweet singing in the choir.

The holly bears a blossom
As white as the lily flower,
And Mary bore sweet Jesus Christ
To be our sweet Saviour:

The holly bears a berry
As red as any blood,
And Mary bore sweet Jesus Christ
To do poor sinners good:

The holly bears a prickle
As sharp as any thorn,
And Mary bore sweet Jesus Christ
On Christmas day in the morn:

The holly bears a bark
As bitter as any gall
And Mary bore sweet Jesus Christ
For to redeem us all:

The holly and the ivy,
When they are both full grown,
Of all the trees that are in the wood,
The holly bears the crown:
ANON

Holly was sacred to Saturn and its glossy red berries thought to symbolize male sexuality. Thanks to its distinctive appearance it was not difficult for the Church to eradicate these pagan beliefs and give the holly a new symbolism: the spiked leaves lent themselves to representing the crown of thorns, and the berries Christ's blood.

Believed to ward off drunkenness, ivy was dedicated to the god Bacchus, who is usually depicted wearing a crown of this versatile evergreen, and carrying an ivy entwined staff. Ivy also symbolized fertility and new life, the female opposite to the holly, though not, apparently, due to its being a 'clinging vine'.

'The Holly and the Ivy' is a splendid English folk carol and was rediscovered by Cecil Sharp towards the end of the century, in Chipping Campden, Gloucestershire.

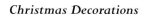

Anon, Gathering
Holly (*card*)

Anon, Children Kissing Under Mistletoe
(*card*)

The Mistletoe (*Viscum album*) is one of a family of parasites. In England it is most abundant on the Apple-tree, more rarely on the Oak. The berries are eaten by most birds, particularly by the Missel-thrush, to which it gives its name. It is through the agency of the birds that the plant is propagated; the viscous nature of the fruit causes it to adhere to the bird's beak, and in the bird's efforts to rid itself of the sticky substance by wiping its beak against a tree, the seeds are transferred to the bark. The Druids held the Mistletoe in great reverence. Pliny says they esteemed it as a gift sent from heaven and held the tree on which it was found as sacred. He says too they called it 'All-heal'. ■

NATURE NOTES

Highly valued by both the Druids and the Norsemen, the mistletoe is surrounded by myth and legend. Most valued when growing on an oak, it had to be cut left-handed with a golden sickle by a fasting Druid clothed in a white tunic. And not only that, for if its ability to promote fertility and ward off witches was to be preserved, the mistletoe was not to be touched by iron or allowed to fall to the ground. Consequently it was caught in a white cloth held by virgins. Harvesting this valuable commodity was no sinecure and woe betide the maiden who let her mind wander at the vital moment.

The Norsemen believed that a truce could be struck between those that met beneath it – a belief, along with that in its ability to promote fertility, which might well have influenced its later and more lighthearted significance at Christmas.

MISTLETOE

Sitting under the mistletoe
(Pale-green, fairy mistletoe),
One last candle burning low
All the sleepy dancers gone,
Just one candle burning on,
Shadows lurking everywhere:
Some one came, and kissed me there.

Tired I was; my head would go
Nodding under the mistletoe
(Pale-green, fairy mistletoe),
No footsteps came, no voice, but only,
Just as I sat there, sleepy, lonely,
Stooped in the still and shadowy air
Lips unseen – and kissed me there.

WALTER DE LA MARE

No one knows who first started the tradition of kissing under the mistletoe – a young blade's good excuse? – but it is a habit peculiar to Britain. A berry would be plucked along with each kiss until the branch was bare.

A bestseller, the song 'Winter Evergreens' must have been a favourite of musical evenings at home.

WINTER EVERGREENS

The roses long have past their prime,
The fruits no more are seen,
So let us chime a Christmas rhyme to hail the Evergreen – the Evergreen!

Though bright may be the summer wreath,
To mourn it were but folly,
While friends delight to meet beneath the Mistletoe –
*   the Mistletoe and Holly!*

Then circle round the ruddy blaze,
And let but mirth be seen,
We still can raise, a song of praise to hail – to hail the Evergreen!

What though we rove the woods no more,
Should we not still be gay,
When Winter hoar, has leaves in the store that never fade away?
Some love to sing the joys of spring,
With them why need we quarrel,
While jovial Christmas deigns to bring the Ivy – the Ivy and the Laurel?

Then let us all each other aid,
Where friendship's wreath is seen,
'Tis never made, of flowers that fade,
But of the Evergreen,
Tis never made of flowers that fade,
But of the Evergreen!

J.E. CARPENTER

William Thackeray seems to have suffered particularly ill luck when it came to his turn to pluck a gift from the tree.

THE SPARKLING BOUGH

The kindly Christmas tree, from which I trust every gentle reader has pulled a bonbon or two, is yet all aflame whilst I am writing, and sparkles with the sweet fruits of its season. You young ladies, may you have plucked pretty giftlings from it; and out of the cracker sugar-plum which you have split with the captain or the sweet young curate may you have read one of those delicious conundrums which the confectioners introduce into the sweetmeats, and which apply to the cunning passion of Love. Those riddles are to be read at *your* age, when I dare say they are amusing. As for Dolly, Merry, and Bell, who are standing at the tree, they don't care about the love-riddle part, but understand the sweet-almond portion very well. They are four, five, six years old. Patience, little people! A dozen merry Christmasses more, and you will be reading those wonderful love-conundrums, too. As for us elderly folks, we watch the babies at their sport, and the young people pulling at the branches: and instead of finding bonbons or sweeties in the packets which *we* pluck off the boughs, *we* find Mr Carnifex's review of the quarter's meat; Mr Sartor's compliments, and little statement for self and the young gentlemen; and Madame de Sainte-Crinoline's respects to the young ladies, who encloses her account, and will send on Saturday, please; or we stretch out our hand to the educational branch of the Christmas tree, and there find a lively and amusing article from the Reverend Henry Holyshade, containing our dear Tommy's exceedingly moderate account for the last term's school expenses. ∎

W.M. THACKERAY

John Callcott Horsley, Decorating with Holly

So now is come our joyful'st feast
Let every man be jolly;
Each room with ivy leaves is drest
And every post with holly.
And while thus inspired we sing,
Let all the streets with echoes ring
Woods and hills and everything
Bear witness we are merry.

GEO. WITHER

Anon, Gathering Holly and Mistletoe (*card*)

Here is a jolly idea from America for the Christmas bride-to-be. Will she be disappointed though, by the small size of the 'shower' gifts? Even a nutmeg grater might prove too heavy for the branches of most trees!

A CHRISTMAS TREE SHOWER

For the bride who announces her engagement in December, a Christmas tree shower might be given Christmas week. Send out cards of invitation in the shape of small Christmas trees, or else paste or paint little evergreen trees on white cards. Ask the guests to bring something small enough to be hung on a little Christmas tree. The bride should be asked to come a little later than the others, so that they may have time to hang their gifts on the tree.

The tree may be as elaborate as you wish to make it. Where trees are hard to procure, a cunning little one on a table is quite large enough. It can be decked with gold and silver hearts and candy kisses, and on its branches should hang the shower gifts, prettily wrapped and tied.

When the bride arrives, she must strip the tree. Among its treasures may be English walnut shells, gilded and tied together, with fortune verses inside. The hostess provides one of these for each guest.

The refreshments may consist of sandwiches cut in the shape of Christmas trees and filled with green pepper and cream cheese; caraway cookies cut in the shape of Christmas trees; and hot chocolate, with a sprig of evergreen tied by a tiny bow of red to each cup-handle.

This affair could be planned specifically as a handkerchief, hosiery or kitchen shower. ■

EMILY ROSE BURT, *ENTERTAINING MADE EASY*

The decoration of the Christmas tree has a pleasing, ritual, quality about it, as favourite and forgotten decorations are once again greeted with joy. But a few always seem to have suffered from lying in a box throughout the year and new, exciting, items are needed. Why not gilded walnuts?

Anon, Decorated Christmas Tree (*card*)

THE CHRISTMAS TREE

This fairy tree for the little ones is so well known that we need scarcely describe it here. It affords a delightful opportunity for the members of the same home to give presents to each other or to their friends; and we believe, that in this volume many kinds of elegant work will be found suggested, exactly suited for the branches of a Christmas tree. A doll well dressed, tiny dolls in the costumes of other lands, paper work, &c., &c., are all adapted to it. Painting flags for it will employ the boys of the house on wet days, and we would suggest that those flags should be *real* ones in form and colour, though not in size.

One very great ornament of a Christmas tree is a gilt walnut. A good number hanging from the branches has an admirable effect, and they are greatly relished by the little ones to whose lot they may fall. To gild walnuts: hammer a rather long tack or nail into the end of the walnut to hold it by, and afterwards to suspend it to the tree. Wash the nut all over with white of egg laid on with a feather. Then roll it in leaf gold till it is well covered. Mind you do not breathe over the leaf gold, or it will fly away from you. When the nut is dry, suspend it to the tree by a red or purple ribbon, the narrowest width you can get. ■

THE GIRL'S HOME COMPANION

The first sight of the Christmas tree, lit by candles and hung with all sorts of glittering and tasty things, never fails to inspire a sense of wonder in a young child whose eye drinks in its beauty and stores away the memory. No matter whether it is first seen by a little girl in Russia before the Revolution or by a little girl at home near Birmingham, the memory is magical.

Towards the end of dinner Yura and Seryozha excused themselves and disappeared into the ballroom. Soon after, Babushka suggested we should leave the table and move towards the closed doors. There we stood waiting. There was an air of expectation. Then, at the tinkling of a bell, all the lights went out, plunging the rooms in darkness. The double-doors were flung wide open.

And there, against the background of total darkness stood this glorious thing, stretching up to the ceiling, ablaze with lights. I had not seen before a Christmas tree of any kind. The sudden impact of this amazing sight overwhelmed me.

Everything shimmered and trembled. The beautiful fairy standing on tiptoes, the snow queen on the sledge driving the silver reindeer to her ice castle with the little boy behind her, Red Riding Hood with her basket setting off to visit her grandma, the little mermaid swaying gently on the edge of a branch, the princess in her gown and diamond coronet, the evil witch standing beside the cottage which is slowly circling on hens' feet, the gnomes and the little winged angels, the tinkling crystal icicles and the sparkling scattered frost. And over all the glitter, the characters out of fairy tales, the apples, sweets and golden walnuts, there was the brilliance of candles, each pointed flame surrounded by a golden halo encircling the tree, layer upon layer of them, and fusing together into one cascading light of dazzling splendour.

I still remember saying to myself, 'This must be like the heaven about which Babushka told me – the place where little children sometimes went to, where they were always happy and never scolded, where everything was bright and golden apples grew on trees.'

Happiness is relative – in my days I have had my share, but nothing has ever surpassed those few rare moments of sheer rapture when I stood gazing up at the wondrous sight of my first Christmas tree. ■

EUGENE FRAZER, *HOUSE ON THE DVINA*

The writer E.V. Lucas, who contributed many humorous pieces to *Punch*, here perfectly captures the tensions and petty jealousies aroused by the honoured task of decorating the church at Christmas.

THE DECORATIONS

The Revd Lawrence Lidbetter to his curate, the Revd Arthur Starling

Dear Starling, I am sorry to appear to be running away at this busy season, but a sudden call to London on business leaves me no alternative. I shall be back on Christmas Eve for certain, perhaps before. You must keep an eye on the decorations, and see that none of our helpers get out of hand. Yours,

L.L.

Mrs Clibborn to the Revd Lawrence Lidbetter

Dear Rector, I think we have got over the difficulty which we were talking of – Mr Lulham's red hair and the discord it would make with the crimson decorations. Maggie and Popsy and I have been working like slaves, and have put up a beautiful and effectual screen of evergreen which completely obliterates the keyboard and organist. I think you will be delighted. Mr Starling approves most cordially. Yours sincerely,

MARY CLIBBORN

Miss Pitt to the Revd Lawrence Lidbetter

My dear Mr Lidbetter, We are all so sorry you have been called away, a strong guiding hand being never more needed. You will remember that it was arranged that I should have sole charge of the

memorial window to Colonel Soper – we settled it just outside the Post Office on the morning that poor Blades was kicked by the Doctor's pony. Well, Miss Lockie now says that Colonel Soper's window belongs to her, and she makes it impossible for me to do anything. I must implore you to write to her putting it right, or the decorations will be ruined. Mr Starling is kind, but quite useless. Yours sincerely,

VIRGINIA PITT

Miss Lockie to the Revd Lawrence Lidbetter

My dear Mr Lidbetter, I am sorry to have to trouble you in your enforced rest, but the interests of the church must not be neglected, and you ought to know that Miss Pitt not only insists that the decoration of Colonel Soper's window was entrusted to her, but prevents me carrying it out. If you recollect, it was during tea at Mrs Millstone's that it was arranged that I should be responsible for

Lucien Pissarro, Snow Scene

this window. A telegram to Miss Pitt would put the matter right at once. Dear Mr Starling is always so nice, but he does so lack firmness. Yours sincerely,

MABEL LOCKIE

Mrs Millstone to the Revd Lawrence Lidbetter

Dear Rector, Just a line to tell you of a delightful device I have hit upon for the decorations. Cottonwool, of course, makes excellent snow, and rice is some-

times used, on gum, to suggest winter too. But I have discovered that the most perfect illusion of a white rime can be obtained by wetting the leaves and then sprinkling flour on them. I am going to get all the others to let me finish off everything like that on Christmas Eve (like varnishing-day at the Academy, my husband says), when it will all be fresh for Sunday. Mr Starling who is proving himself such a dear, is delighted with the scheme. I hope you are well in that dreadful foggy city. Yours sincerely,

ADA MILLSTONE

Mrs Hobbs, charwoman, to the Revd Lawrence Lidbetter

Honoured Sir, I am writing to you because Hobbs and me dispare of getting any justice from the so called ladies who have been turning the holy Church of St Michael and all Angels into a Covent Garden market. To sweep up all holly and green stuff I don't mind, because I have heard you say year after year that we should all do our best at Christmas to help each other. I always hold that charity and kindness are more than rubys, but when it comes to flour I say no. If you would believe it, Mrs Millstone is first watering the holly and the lorrel to make it wet, and then sprinkling flour on it to look like hore frost, and the mess is something dreadful, all over the cushions and carpet. To sweep up ordinary dust I don't mind, more particularly as it is my paid work and bounden duty; but unless it is made worth my while Hobbs says I must say no. We draw the line at sweeping up dough. Mr Starling is very kind, but as Hobbs says you are the founting head. Awaiting a reply, I am, your humble servant,

MARTHA HOBBS

Mr Lulham, organist, to the Revd Lawrence Lidbetter

Dear Sir, I shall be glad to have a line from you authorising me to insist upon the removal of a large screen of evergreens which Mrs Clibborn and her daughters have erected by the organ. There seems to be an idea that the organ is unsightly, although we have had no complaints hitherto, and the effect of this barrier will be to interfere very seriously with the choral part of the service. Mr Starling sympathises with me, but has not taken any steps. Believe me, yours faithfully,

WALTER LULHAM

The Revd Lawrence Lidbetter to Mrs Lidbetter

My Dearest Harriet, I am having, as I expected, an awful time with the decorations, and I send you a batch of letters and leave the situation to you. Miss Pitt had better keep the Soper window. Give the Lockie girl one of the autograph copies of my *Narrow Path*, with a reference underneath my name to the chapter on self-sacrifice, and tell her how sorry I am that there has been a misunderstanding. Mrs Hobbs must have an extra half-crown, and the flouring must be discreetly discouraged – on the ground of waste of food material. Assure Lulham that there shall be no barrier, and then tell Mrs Clibborn that the organist has been given a pledge that nothing should intervene between his music and the congregation. I am dining with the Lawsons tonight, and we go afterwards to the *Tempest*, I think. Your devoted,

E.V. LUCAS, *PUNCH*

For those skilled in stencilling, a stencilled Christmas border, to decorate a room, swagged and ribboned, would well reward the effort of execution and if painted in watercolour need not be a permanent feature.

BORDERS IN INTERIORS

Border stencils have a multitude of uses, from the familiar horizontal border at picture rail or ceiling height to the more flamboyant border around a door or window. In decorating a room a border can be used discreetly to unite disparate elements in the decorative scheme, as well as creating a focus of attention that can alter the impression of space in a room.

Scale and colour also have an important part to play in this. A delicate border that is only 2–3in/5–7cm deep will be virtually invisible at a height of 10ft/9.5m. A change of colour or a change of scale may be needed to make it more conspicuous. Alternatively a large border like a swag may need a high ceiling to do it justice.

INCORPORATING TIES IN DESIGN

Making a stencil out of any design reduces it to a flat outline. This is because of the necessity for ties or bridges in the stencil to maintain its shape. A suggestion of form can be conveyed either by overprinting the design with subsequent stencil plates, to remove the flattening effect of the ties, or by shading the paint carefully across the stencil. The illustration shows both these methods of printing.

What could be a more welcome gift than a Christmas decoration to those either too busy or unable to make their own?

Table decorations are particularly colourful and last a considerable time, with the added advantage that after dining they still look attractive on a shelf or window-sill. Simple bowls of holly, with dried leaves or silk flowers, pine cones or tree bark, can be used to create a Christmas display of traditional colours. Candlesticks can also be decorated (using mastic) to anchor sprays and garlands into position. But be careful, for dried flowers can be very inflammable, so use tall candles and artificial berries, beads and tinsel. The colours of winter and Christmas time are red and green: red ribbon, candles and berries, green leaves of holly, laurel and fir Christmas trees. Their inherent richness conveys the comfort of traditional values. ■

CHRISTMAS RIBBON TABLE CENTRE
MEASUREMENTS
Base 8in (20cm) diameter

MATERIALS
Offray ribbons: $2\frac{1}{4}$yd (2m) of $1\frac{1}{2}$in (39mm) width Red
$3\frac{1}{4}$yd (3m) of $\frac{3}{8}$in (15mm) width Green
$39\frac{1}{2}$in (1m) of $\frac{1}{8}$in (3mm) width White and Silver Lurex
Florist's wires, stub wires, silver rose wires
3 pine cones
3 red glass Christmas tree balls
3 silver glass Christmas tree balls
3 teasles
Seed heads, eg poppy and nigella (love-in-a-mist)
Gold spray paint (it is important to purchase gold paint especially manufactured for these purposes for health reasons)
$1\frac{5}{8}$yd (1.5mm) cream lace
1 cake board 8in (20cm) diameter (covered with green fabric optional)
Glue
Small block of Styrofoam
1 candle
Cocktail sticks

TO MAKE
Following diagram A as a guide, together with picture above:
1 Make multiple loop bows with green and silver ribbons securing each with silver rose wire. Diagram B
2 Place stub wire around lower part of each pine cone and twist ends together.
3 Place stub wire through the hanging loop of each glass ball and twist ends together ready to place in styrofoam block.

DIAGRAM A

4 Spray cones, teasles and seed heads with gold paint and leave to dry.
5 Staple ring of lace to edge of cake board a little way in from edge.
6 Gather and secure with a florist's stub wire the remaining lace to form small cockades.
7 Glue styrofoam to centre of base.
8 Sellotape several cocktail sticks to end of candle and insert candle to centre of styrofoam.
9 Arrange other materials around candle and ribbon bows to completely cover styrofoam.
10 Artificial holly and mistletoe can be added.
When making multiple bows, make as many loops as required, all of equal size.

Lighting can give atmosphere, creating the correct mood for the occasion. It will vary depending on the activities the room accommodates. In dining areas lighting can generally be lower, but nothing can evoke the mood of Christmas more than the light of candles, which create a close intimacy. Who could resist sitting down to Christmas dinner at this table? Certainly good food and wine are in evidence, but anyone who loves traditional styling will approve of this scene: a decorative festive table-cloth, sweetmeats and holly berries reflecting the candlelight, bathing the scene with the shadows of the season, warming the room and creating a cosiness that befits the occasion. The family is reminded at dinner of past good times, bringing, symbolically at least, the spirit of Christmas to this festive meal with friends and family. ∎

The Scandinavians burn candles in their homes through the dark winter months, rightly believing that their soft glow not only lights up the home but also feeds the otherwise flagging spirit. Their soft, warm, light certainly creates a heartwarming atmosphere like no other.

A glowing display of dried flowers and cones sprayed with gold paint makes an eye-catching feature whether at the centre of a dining table, sparkling in the candlelight, or elsewhere.

A CHRISTMAS DISPLAY

YOU WILL NEED
A basket
12 fir cones (choose different shapes and sizes)
3 dried peony heads in full bloom
6 hydrangea flowers
3 stems of Chinese lantern pods
Dried grasses
Eucalyptus pods
Adiantum fern
Gold (or silver) spray paint

Christmas displays are traditionally made with evergreens, cones and red berries, but I think it is fun to break with tradition occasionally and to create a display that will be completely different yet retain the feel of this special day. This basket is made by spraying all the dried-flower material with gold paint.

Take plenty of newspaper and place it on the floor or over a large work surface. If you have a garden, it would be even better to spray these things outdoors to avoid any mess and to avoid inhaling the spray paint. If you do spray inside, remember to ensure that there is good ventilation from an open window or door.

Place one type of dried material on the paper and spray it as evenly as possible. Leave to dry for a few minutes – it will be fairly quick if you do not saturate the plants – then turn it over and spray the other side. Do the same to the other plants. When all the plant material has been sprayed and is completely dry, arrange it in the basket, preferably into a base of Drihard clay, which will give weight to the basket and help to prevent the material from becoming top heavy. This arrangement could be packed away after Christmas and brought out in subsequent years. ■

POMANDERS

YOU WILL NEED

2 oranges

8–10oz (250–300g) whole, large-headed cloves

1oz (30g) orris-root powder

4oz (125g) cinnamon powder

1oz (30g) powdered cloves

1oz (30g) ground nutmeg

1oz (30g) allspice

2 whole cinnamon sticks

1 drop bergamot oil

1 drop lemon verbena oil

12in (30cm), $\frac{1}{2}$in (12mm) ribbon for hanging the pomander (optional)

36in (90cm), $\frac{1}{2}$in (12mm) ribbon for winding around the pomander and for the bow

18in (45cm) plain ribbon tape

A knitting needle

A fork

A box of large-headed pins

A large china mixing bowl

A wooden spoon

A length of muslin

String

A piece of newspaper (optional)

Pomanders were originally carried by those traversing the fetid and unhealthy streets of towns in the Middle Ages. They not only warded off foul odours but were also thought to keep disease at bay. They can sweetly scent a room as well as look decorative.

Finished and cured pomanders, decorated with festive ribbons.

BELOW RIGHT: *Two rose bud pomanders, decorated with ribbons and ready for use, and, on the right, a foam ball showing how the rose buds should be positioned.*

There are two types of pomander, which are not only attractive but are easy to make and very effective. The first is a pomander made from citrus fruit pierced with cloves and left to cure in a number of spices. These are traditionally regarded as Christmas pomanders, but I have a large bowl filled with them in my dining-room and it gives the most wonderful fragrance all through the year. Making pomanders like this is something that children enjoy doing enormously, and with many pairs of willing hands to help you will have them made in no time!

Although these pomanders can be made from any citrus fruit, I think my favourites are those made with oranges. Choose small oranges if possible – they require less filling and are more economical on ribbon. The ribbons can be any type and colour, but I think they look particularly attractive using either tartan or velvet ribbon.

The recipe below is for two orange pomanders. If you wish to make a larger quantity, say six pomanders, double the

quantities. The fragrance of your finished pomander, will last for years, although they do shrink in size. If you need to revive the fragrance, run the pomander under warm water, remove excess water and replace it in the curing mixture for several weeks, and it will smell as wonderful as ever. These pomanders will bring fresh, new fragrance to drawers, wardrobes or any enclosed space.

Unless your working surface is Formica or some similar material, I suggest that you put down newspaper before you begin. Place the ribbon tape around the orange, keeping it as even as possible; if you wish, you can place a second tape around the orange to create four different sections. Place pins 2in (5cm) apart in each side of the tape so that it does not slip out of position. When you have finished inserting the cloves, remove the tape, leaving channels for the ribbon.

Pierce the surface of the orange with a knitting needle; cloves tend to be rather hard to push in by themselves and sometimes break with the pressure. After the initial hole, it is

often quicker to use a four-pronged fork, which will leave the correct spaces between each clove. Complete the first circuit, working close to the tape, which you should use as a guide line, then add a second row, leaving a small gap between the rows. Continue until both oranges are evenly covered. When you are satisfied with the results, mix the spices in a bowl, eliminating any lumps, add the drops of oil and, having removed the tape, place the pomanders in this mixture, turn them, and, using a wooden spoon, place some of the powder on top of them. Cover the bowl with muslin and place it in a warm, dry place. Turn the pomanders every day; they sometimes take up to six weeks to be completely cured, so if you are planning to use them at Christmas-time, you will have to make a start in early November.

To decorate the pomanders, gently brush off any excess powder – a very soft toothbrush is good for this purpose – and bind the ribbon around the channels. Tie a knot and make a bow. If you wish to suspend them, place some ribbon through the top, tying it securely to the first pieces, and then another knot at the ribbon ends. ■

ROSE BUD POMANDERS

YOU WILL NEED
A small plastic foam (Oasis) sphere
4–6oz (125–180g) scented rose buds
Several medium gauge stubb wires, 6in (15cm) long
Wire cutters
Scissors
12in (30cm) medium width satin ribbon for the bow
36in (90cm) narrow satin ribbon for suspending
and decorating
Glue

This type of pomander can be made using virtually any type of dried flower, but I think rose bud pomanders are the prettiest. The buds usually have convenient little stalks to place into the sphere, and it is possible to find shops that will sell the scented rose buds in the form of pot-pourri. The spheres will smell wonderful and can be hung or placed in wardrobes, drawers or linen cupboards, or suspended in a room, such as on a dressing-table mirror or from a bed post. They look simply beautiful when decorated with matching satin ribbon and make the most delightful gift, looking particularly pretty when placed in a delicately designed box filled with pastel tissue paper. ■

An ideal gift or especially made to wear on Christmas day, this holly design sweater will keep cheeks rosy throughout the winter season.

HOLLY SWEATER – CHILD'S

Sizes

To fit chest 51[56:61:66]cm, 20[22:24:26]ins
Actual chest 56.5[60:66.5:70]cm, $22\frac{1}{4}[23\frac{3}{4}:26\frac{1}{4}:27\frac{1}{2}]$ins
Length 36[38:40:42]cm, $14\frac{1}{4}[15: 15\frac{3}{4}:16\frac{1}{2}]$ins
Sleeve seam 30[33:33:36]cm, $11\frac{3}{4}[13:13:14\frac{1}{4}]$ins

Materials

3[4:4:5] × 50g balls of Emu Superwash OR Supermatch DK in main colour (A) 1 ball each in 2 contrast colours (B and C) One Pair each $3\frac{1}{4}$mm (US3) and 4mm (US6) knitting needles

Tension/Gauge 23 sts and 26 rows to 10cm, 4 ins over st st using 4mm (US6) needles

BACK

☆☆Using 3¼mm (US3) needles and A, cast on 61[65:69:73]sts.

Cont in K1, P1 rib as foll:

1st row: K1, ☆P1, K1, rep from ☆ to end.

2nd row: P1, ☆K1, P1, rep from ☆ to end. Rep these 2 rows for 5cm, 2 ins, ending with a 2nd row.

Inc row: Rib 12[13:9:8], ☆inc in next st, rib 11[12:6:7], rep from ☆ to last 13[13:11:9]sts, inc in next st, rib to end. 65[69:77:81]sts.

Change to 4mm (US6) needles and beg with a P row, work 7[3:9:7] rows st st.

Commence patt.

1st row: (RS) K1B, ☆3A, 1B, rep from ☆ to end.

2nd row: P1A, ☆1B, 3A, rep from ☆ to end.

3rd row: ☆K2A, 1B, 1A, rep from ☆ to last st, 1A.

4th row: P1A, ☆2A, 1B, 1A, rep from ☆ to end.

5th row: ☆K1C, 3A, rep from ☆ to last st, 1C.

6th row: P1A, ☆1A, 1C, 2A, rep from ☆ to end.

7th row: ☆K2A, with C, cast on 2sts, cast off 2 sts to make bobble, 1A, rep from ☆ to last st, 1A.

8th row: P1C, ☆3A, 1C, rep from ☆ to end.

9th row: ☆K1A, 1B, 2A, rep from ☆ to last st, 1A.

10th row: P1A, ☆1A, 1B, 2A, rep from ☆ to end.

11th row: ☆K3A, 1B, rep from ☆ to last st, 1A.

12th row: P1B, ☆3A, 1B, rep from ☆ to end.

Cont in A only. Work 6[8:8:12] rows st st.

These 18[20:20:24]rows form the patt.

Cont in patt until work measures 21cm, 8½ins from beg, ending with a WS row.

Shape armholes

Cast off 4 sts at beg of next 2 rows. 57[61:69:73]sts. ☆☆

Cont in patt until work measures 36[38:40:42]cm. 14¼[15:15¾:16½]ins from beg, ending with a WS row

Shape shoulders

Cast off 14[16:18:20] sts at beg of next 2 rows. Leave rem 29[29: 33:33] sts on a spare needle.

FRONT

Work as given for back from ☆☆ to ☆☆. Cont in patt until work measures 30[32:34:36]cm, 11¾[12½:13½:14¼]ins from beg, ending with a WS row.

Shape neck

Next row: Patt 24[26:29:31] sts and turn leaving rem sts on a spare needle.

Complete left side of neck first.

Cast off 4 sts at beg of next row, 3 sts at beg of foll alt row, then 2 sts at beg of next alt row. Dec 1 st at neck edge on foll 1[1:2:2] alt rows. 14[16:18:20] sts.

Cont without further shaping until work measures same as back to shoulder shaping, ending at armhole edge.

Shape shoulder

Cast off rem sts.

With RS of work facing, return to sts on spare needle. Sl centre 9[9:11:11] sts onto a holder, rejoin yarn at neck edge, patt to end.

Patt 1 row. Complete as given for first side of neck.

SLEEVES

Using 3¼mm (US3) needles and A,

cast on 33[37:43:47]sts.

Work in K1, P1 rib as given for back for 5cm, 2ins, ending with a 1st row. P1 row.

Now cont in patt as given for back. Inc and work into patt 1 st at each end of every 3rd row until there are 69[77:87:97] sts.

Cont without shaping until work measures 32[35:35:38]cm, 12½[13¾:13¾:15]ins from beg, ending with a WS row. Cast off loosely.

TO MAKE UP/TO FINISH

Join right shoulder seam.

NECKBAND

With RS of work facing, using 3¼mm (US3) needles and A, K up 22 sts down left side of neck, K across 9[9:11:11] sts at centre front, K up 23 sts up right side of neck, then K across 29[29:33:33] sts on back neck. 83[83:89:89] sts.

Beg with a 2nd row, work in K1, P1 rib as given for back for 5cm, 2ins. Cast off loosely in rib.

Join left shoulder and neckband seam, fold neckband in half onto WS and slip stitch in place. Placing centre of cast off edge to shoulder seams, set in sleeves, joining final rows to cast off sts at underarms. Join side and sleeve seams.

WHIRLING SNOWFLAKES – CHRISTMAS TREE RIBBON DECORATIONS

Homemade Christmas tree decorations such as these Whirling Snowflakes will be a welcome introduction to the Christmas tree 'box'; they are not only unbreakable, they will also add that all-important personal touch. There are so many lovely ribbons to choose from to-day that none of these Whirling Snowflakes needs look alike.

RIBBON SNOWBALLS
MATERIALS
Selection of Offray ribbons, such as fancy Jacquards, metallic ribbons, satins, stripes and spots

Styrofoam balls available from craft shops
Pins
(Beads and sequins optional)

TO MAKE
1 Choose a ribbon and pin one end to top of snowball.
2 Take ribbon round the ball, pinning at bottom as you go.
3 Pin again on top.
4 Choose next ribbon to go round ball. Mix colours and patterns of ribbons. Do not fill all the spaces – let some of the white snowball show between ribbons. Try pinning narrower ribbons over wide ribbons.
5 Pin zigzags of ribbons up and down round the ball (optional).
6 Pin ribbons horizontally round the ball.
7 Slip beads or sequins on to the pin before pushing it into the ribbon.
8 Pin loops of ribbons to form bows at top of snowball.

9 Pin ribbon loops to tops of balls for hanging.
10 Experiment with different ribbons to create a variety of snowballs.

CHRISTMAS FARE

Christmas dinner, the nourishing heart of the festival, is pleasurably anticipated weeks in advance and remembered long after. It is a time when family and friends gather round the table, and its success relies as much on the goodwill of the company as on its careful preparation.

The menu has changed little over the centuries, except in the choice of meats. A big fat goose or juicy joint of beef were favoured by the Victorians but gradually the recently introduced turkey, a rarity before the 1870s, rose in popularity. A bird big enough to feed a party of friends and family, it not only looked mouth wateringly festive but, accompanied by the customary stuffing and sausages, tasted even better than goose or beef.

Edith Holden's contemporaries had a never-before-or-since-rivalled capacity to consume huge and frequent meals, a simple two courses for lunch or dinner being considered too skimpy and mean to contemplate. Instead, the wealthy household would sit down to at least an eight-course dinner and then, having spent the evening playing bridge or 'Charades' or indulging in social chit-chat, would consume a plate of cold meats or sandwiches.

The following chapter offers some old and new recipes for traditional Christmas fare, ideas on how to create a festive table, and descriptions of how families, both rich and poor, prepared for and enjoyed the feast.

Details on the administration of the home provide a background to the feast, giving an idea of the complexity of everyday living in a household of those times.

The cost of living was cheap in Edith's day and labour plentiful. The Holdens would undoubtedly have employed at least two, perhaps more, servants. Edwardian writers of household and cookery books went into great detail about the careful pecking order of the below-stairs staff and their duties, what went into running an ordered home and 'how to get on in Society'. It was an age littered, more than any other, with rules as to what was correct etiquette and advice on how to carry out even minor tasks abounded. The Edwardian lady's day (if she desired to become a successful society hostess) was far from leisured, and could be likened to running a battleship, but at least there were, too, helpful writers like Mrs Earle and Mrs Peel who, full of common sense, did not let the worry of 'what will the neighbours say' dictate their every move.

Details of the everyday work and wages of the various staff are food for thought. They worked long hours and however kindly the master and mistress, Christmas was a time of greater activity than ever with no hopes of a day's respite. They might well receive a gift from the family but very often this was of a new uniform rather than an indulgent frivolity.

I particularly want to say a last word to housekeepers who are anxious to indulge in hospitality. Hospitality should mean, to my mind, not altering our whole way of living, but giving the best of our habitual food. For this nothing is so telling, whether the dinner be large or small, as the procuring of some special seasonable luxury. It is well worth taking the trouble to get any such luxuries, not from the usual shop in your neighbourhood, but from the very best shop you know of for each speciality, whether fish, game, vegetable, Italian goods more especially, fruit (fresh or bottled), dessert, biscuits, or cake. The really good housekeeper is alert to learn where the best things come from, and to take hints wherever she goes. One should never through idleness give up getting the best things. If you go to the expense of entertaining at all, it makes little difference in the way of money whether you deal at a specially good shop or a second-rate one, and the results at your table are very different indeed . . .

There is no doubt that some women have the gift of being good hostesses, while others have not, and, although it is a sad fact to have to admit in one of the last chapters of a housekeeping book, it is not invariably the best kept house that is the pleasantest. The woman who talks about the servants, fusses about domestic details, becomes fretful if her guests strew their belongings about the rooms or are five minutes late for luncheon, cannot atone for her misdeeds by the comfort of her spare rooms and the excellence of her dinners. The personal charm of the hostess counts for something even among people who are so dependent on luxury as the English upper classes. ■

MRS EARLE, *POT POURRI FROM A SURREY GARDEN*

Arrangement of Work in Fair-sized Country House (3 Servants, Nurse and Groom-Gardener) Large hall, drawing-room, dining-room, morning-room, smoking-room, 3 servants' rooms, box-room, store-room, large offices, 2 nurseries, 1 bed and dressing room, 3 spare rooms and 1 dressing-room. Family – master, mistress, two young children, occasional visitors. Servants – cook, £20; house-parlourmaid, £18; housemaid, £16; nurse, £24; groom and gardener. Meals – breakfast, 8.30; lunch, 1.15; dinner, 7.30.

Cook's Time-Table Down at 6.30; light fire; do hall; serve breakfasts for 8.30; do own cleaning and cooking for remainder of day.

Groom cleans knives and boots, sweeps up back yard, and cleans windows and brushes clothes.

Gardener does pumping, and fills coal-scuttles and brings in wood.

Nurse does own nurseries, with exception of grates and weekly cleaning. Meals and coals carried up for her. Takes entire charge of children; does their needlework and washing of small woollen things.

House-Parlourmaid Down 6.30; do dining-room, and drawing-room, and dust first flight of stairs; get breakfast for 8.30; have own breakfast; do lamps; clear breakfast; go up to bedrooms and do housework until 12.15; dress; wash up; lay lunch, and wait; have own dinner; clear and wash up luncheon things; do pantrywork, sewing, and usual duties of parlourmaid for remainder of day.

Housemaid Down 6.30; light nursery fires; do two sitting-rooms; call, and take hot water; have breakfast; go upstairs and do housework until dinner-time; clean store-room, back stairs, servants' rooms two afternoons a week; other afternoons do light work, such as brass-cleaning, putting away and giving out of linen, etc, and mending; get kitchen tea, see to room as usual, help wait at dinner; take up nursery meals and coals, and trim upstairs, passage, and nursery lamps. ■

Family - Husband and Wife, three Girls (14, 16, 18), two grown-up Sons. Income - £2,000. Place of Abode - Near London.

	£	s.	d.
Rent, taxes, rates	300	0	0
Boys' allowances, £50 each	100	0	0
Governess and classes for girls	100	0	0
Dress and small personal expenses of husband and wife, £100 and £100	200	0	0
Wine	50	0	0
Coal and light	45	0	0
Wages – Manservant, £50; cook, £30; kitchen-maid, £16; two housemaids, £20 and £16; sewing maid, £25	157	0	0
Washing, £2 a week	104	0	0
House bills for fourteen people, at about 12s a head, not including garden produce, flowers and some eggs and poultry, but including dinner parties occasionally	437	0	0
Carried forward	1,493	0	0

MRS C.S. PEEL, *HOW TO KEEP HOUSE*

W. Rainey, Housmaid Polishing the Grate

Jules Alexandre Green, The End of Dinner

Nothing was too much trouble when it came to decorating the Christmas table, both here and in the United States at the turn of the century. Paul Nesbit in his book *Novel Suggestions for Social Occasions* obviously considers the menu of secondary importance, good though it sounds.

A CHRISTMAS DINNER

If one wishes to develop the idea of Santa and his sleigh, buy a doll and dress as Santa and fashion a sleigh out of cardboard and colour red. About Santa and his sleigh, which may be filled with bonbons or tiny gifts like animals from Noah's ark, etc, for the guests, have imitation snow of coarse salt or sugar, or cotton sprinkled with diamond dust. Have tiny sprigs of evergreen standing upright for trees. At each plate have a tiny sleigh filled with red and green candies and light the table with red candles and shades in shape of Christmas bells. Have the dinner cards ornamented with little watercolour Santa Claus' heads or little trees. If one uses the Christmas bell idea have the bells covered with scarlet crêpe tissue and swung from the chandelier. One can have the letters on them spell 'Merry Christmas'. In the centre of the table place a mound of holly with bright red berries; have red candles arranged in any design one chooses, and far enough away so their heat will not ignite the tissue paper bells. White paper shades with sprays of holly painted or tied on make pretty Christmas shades. Have the bonbons, nuts, salads and ice cream served in cases in shape of bells, or have the ice cream frozen in bell shape. If one wishes to decorate with the tiny trees, fasten them upright in flower pots and cover the pots with red paper. Hang bonbons or sparkling objects and tinsel or little favours of bells for the guests from the branches of the trees. The holly wreaths may be used in any way the fancy dictates – a large centre wreath and if the table is round, a second larger one near the edge of the table, leaving room for the plates or single candlesticks set in tiny wreaths at intervals between the larger wreaths. The

PHEASANT SOUP

Any game bird, small or of doubtful age, can be used for this. One large or two small birds make a good dish, served whole, with creamed potatoes and sprouts or broccoli, after the broth.

1 pheasant
2 oz / 50 g / $\frac{1}{2}$ cup flour
1 oz / 25 g / 2 tbsp butter or dripping
4 oz / 125 g / $\frac{1}{2}$ cup chopped lean ham or bacon
2 onions
$\frac{1}{2}$ head of celery
2 pt / 1 1/5 cups water or vegetable stock
salt and ground black pepper to taste
2 oz / 50 g / 1 cup soft breadcrumbs
yolks of 2 hard-boiled eggs
1 small glass sherry or madeira

Joint the bird (unless using as a main course), flour it well and place it in a large pan with the butter, already melted but not brown. Cook gently till the bird is browned, then remove to a warm dish. Add the ham, sliced onions and roughly chopped celery to the pan, and cook in the remaining butter till soft; cover with salted water, bring to the boil and replace the bird, then simmer in the broth for about 2 hours until tender. For a light soup, remove the bird and vegetables carefully, strain the broth, then add the breadcrumbs, mashed egg yolks, and, unless needed for a main course, the finely chopped breast of the bird. Season with pepper and add the sherry before serving.

CHESTNUT SOUP

1 lb / 500 g chestnuts
1 pt / 600 ml / $2\frac{1}{2}$ cups chicken stock
1 pt / 600 ml / $2\frac{1}{2}$ cups milk
1 oz / 25 g / $\frac{1}{4}$ cup cornflour (cornstarch)
salt and cayenne pepper to taste

Prepare the chestnuts by slitting the skins with a knife; then either put them in a hot oven for 15 minutes, and remove the skins; or boil them for 5 minutes in a pan of water and skin them one at a time. Heat the stock and peeled chestnuts, boil, then simmer for about 30 minutes until the chestnuts are soft enough to be either pressed through a coarse sieve, or mashed in the stock – a potato masher is good for this job. In a separate pan, melt the butter, add the cornflour and mix well, then gradually add the warmed milk. Pour this mixture into the chestnut purée, mix all together till smooth, reheat and season with salt and cayenne pepper to taste. For a richer flavour add a piece of butter and a tablespoonful of cream before serving.

different dishes may be garnished with wreaths of parsley, radishes, endive, cress, or the sweets with rings of kisses, macaroons, whipped cream roses, candies, etc.

Here is a suitable menu. Oyster or clam cocktail, wafers, consomme, bouillon or cream of celery soup, celery, radishes, small square crackers. If one wishes a fish course, creamed lobster or salmon with potato balls. Roast turkey or game of any sort, glazed sweet potatoes, corn fritters, creamed peas, peach, currant or grape jelly, hot rolls. Cranberry sherbet; nut salad with plain bread and butter sandwiches, individual plum puddings with burning brandy, ice cream in any desired shape, white cake or fruit cake if one does not have the plum pudding, cheese, crackers, coffee. ∎

PAUL NESBIT, *NOVEL SUGGESTIONS FOR SOCIAL OCCASIONS*

FAMILY DINNERS FOR DECEMBER

1.

SUNDAY – Mock turtle soup. Roast ribs of beef, boned and rolled, Brussels sprouts, potatoes. Mince pies, jelly.

MONDAY – Pea soup. Cold beef, salad, mashed potatoes. Pheasants. Macaroni cheese.

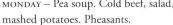

TUESDAY – Cod and oyster sauce. Salmi of pheasants. Stewed beef and vegetables, potatoes. Fig pudding.

WEDNESDAY – Ox-cheek soup. Saddle of mutton, Brussels sprouts, potatoes. Lemon pudding.

THURSDAY – Oyster soup. Cold mutton, beetroot, mashed potatoes. Snipe. Cheese.

FRIDAY – Fried soles. Roast loin of pork, greens, potatoes. Cabinet pudding.

SATURDAY – Soup. Mutton rissoles, cold port, salad, mashed potatoes. Cold pudding warmed with wine sauce.

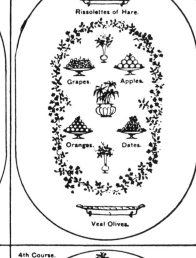

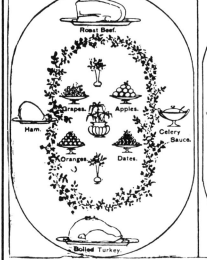

2.

SUNDAY – Roast turkey, sausages, greens, potatoes. Plum pudding, mince pies. Cheese. Dessert.

MONDAY – Oyster soup. Beef olives. Cold turkey, mashed potatoes. Slices of cold plum pudding, baked in a custard.

TUESDAY – Fried soles. Boiled mutton, turnips, potatoes, caper sauce. Apple charlotte.

WEDNESDAY – Croquettes of turkey. Cold mutton hashed, fried potatoes. Marmalade pudding.

THURSDAY – Roast beef, horseradish sauce, greens, potatoes. Baked batter pudding, with apples.

FRIDAY – Cod's head and shoulders, oyster sauce.

Cold beef, baked potatoes, beetroot. Mince pies.

SATURDAY – Mulligatawny soup. Ragout of cold beef, potatoes. Mansfield pudding. ∎

MRS BEETON'S *BOOK OF HOUSEHOLD MANAGEMENT*

ROAST GOOSE

A well roasted goose makes a splendid alternative to the Christmas turkey, although tradition has it that the young bird tastes best in the autumn, at Michael-mas. The bird's giblets make a delicious stew, and it is a good idea to save the surplus fat, which is very good for cooking and as a preservative for cold meat. Plenty of fruit in the stuffing, and a good apple sauce, will help to counteract the richness of the bird. Alternatively make chestnut forcemeat (page 99); when mixing the cooked liver with the chestnuts add also:

$\frac{1}{2}$*lb / 225 g / 1 cup sausagemeat*
2 sticks /$\frac{1}{2}$ cup chopped celery

Clean and dry the bird thoroughly, then stuff it and truss it for roasting. It may be wrapped in foil if you prefer and should be basted well from time to time with the fat and juices; these will need spooning into a separate basin, since there is always a lot of fat from a goose. Allow 15 minutes cooking time for each 1 lb/450 g of the bird's weight, plus 15 minutes over. Cook in a moderate oven (375°F/190°C/Mark 5).

SOYER'S RECIPE FOR GOOSE STUFFING

Mode – Take 4 apples, peeled and cored, 4 onions, 4 leaves of sage and 4 leaves of lemon thyme not broken, and boil them in a stewpan with sufficient water to cover them; when done, pulp them through a sieve, removing the sage and thyme; then add sufficient pulp of mealy potatoes to cause it to be sufficiently dry, without sticking to the hand; add pepper and salt, and stuff the bird.

MRS BEETON'S *BOOK OF HOUSEHOLD MANAGEMENT*

A CHRISTMAS CAROL

Such a bustle ensued that you might have thought a goose the rarest of all birds; a feathered phenomenon, to which a black swan was a matter of course – and in truth it was something very like it in that house. Mrs Cratchit made the gravy (ready beforehand in a little saucepan) hissing hot; Master Peter mashed the potatoes with incredible vigour; Miss Belinda sweetened up the apple-sauce; Martha dusted the hot plates; Bob took Tiny Tim beside him in a tiny corner at the table; the two young Cratchits set chairs for everybody, not forgetting themselves, and mounting guard upon their posts, crammed spoons into their mouths, lest they should shriek for goose before their turn came to be helped. At last the dishes were set on, and grace was said. It was succeeded by a breathless pause, as Mrs Cratchit, looking slowly all along the carving-knife, prepared to plunge it in the breast; but when she did, and when the long expected gush of stuffing issued forth, one murmur of delight arose all round the board, and even Tiny Tim, excited by the two young Cratchits, beat on the table with the handle of his knife, and feebly cried Hurrah!

There never was such a goose. Bob said he didn't believe there ever was such a goose cooked. Its tenderness and flavour, size and cheapness, were the themes of universal admiration. Eked out by apple-sauce and mashed potatoes, it was sufficient dinner for the whole family; indeed, as Mrs Cratchit said with great delight (surveying one small atom of a bone upon the dish), they hadn't ate it all at last! Yet every one had had enough, and the youngest Cratchits in particular, were steeped in sage and onion to the eyebrows! But now, the plates being changed by Miss Belinda, Mrs Cratchit left the room alone – too nervous to bear witnesses – to take the pudding up and bring it in.

Suppose it should not be done enough! Suppose it should break in turning out! Suppose somebody should have got over the wall of the back-yard, and stolen it, while they were merry with the goose – a supposition at which the two young Cratchits became livid! All sorts of horrors were supposed.

Hallo! A great deal of steam! The pudding was out of the copper. A smell like a washing-day! That was the cloth. A smell like an eating-house and a pastrycook's next door to each other, with a laundress's next door to that! That was the pudding! In half a minute Mrs Cratchit entered – flushed, but smiling proudly – with the pudding, like a speckled cannon-ball, so hard and firm, blazing in half of half-a-quartern of ignited brandy, and bedight with Christmas holly stuck into the top.

Oh, a wonderful pudding! Bob Cratchit said, and calmly too, that he regarded it as the greatest success achieved by Mrs Cratchit since their marriage. Mrs Cratchit said that now the weight was off her mind, she would confess she had had her doubts about the quantity of flour. Everybody had something to say about it, but nobody said or thought it was at all a small pudding for a large family. It would have been flat heresy to do so. Any Cratchit would have blushed to hint at such a thing.

At last the dinner was all done, the cloth was cleared, the hearth swept, and the fire made up. The compound in the jug being tasted, and considered perfect, apples and oranges were put upon the table, and a shovel-full of chestnuts on the fire. Then all the Cratchit family drew round the hearth, in what Bob Cratchit called a circle, meaning half a one; and at Bob Cratchit's elbow stood the family display of glass. Two tumblers, and a custard-cup without a handle.

These held the hot stuff from the jug, however, as well as golden goblets would have done; and Bob served it out with beaming looks, while the chestnuts on the fire sputtered and cracked noisily. Then Bob proposed: 'A Merry Christmas to us all, my dears. God bless us!' Which all the family re-echoed. ■

CHARLES DICKENS, *A CHRISTMAS CAROL*

Was there ever such a happy-sounding Christmas dinner, as this one, far from lavish but still encompassing the best traditions of the feast? One can almost smell the goose and feel the heat of the steaming pudding.

Mission work by the middle and upper classes was a feature of the Edwardian life, many giving an evening a week to entertain or educate the 'lower orders'. It was thought to keep them out of the public houses and trouble generally, though it was ultimately government legislation rather than charity that improved the life of the legions of poor and underpaid. But who in straitened circumstances would not relish a 'lordly' – and free – feast?

To 970 poor families in the Mile End district, Christmas will be a day of rejoicing and plenty. Through the generosity of the Mr F.N. Charrington's Tower Hamlets Mission they were supplied last night with a dinner 'fit for a Lord' as some of them put it.

DAILY CHRONICLE, **25 DECEMBER 1906**

It isn't so much what's on the table that matters, as what's on the chairs.

W.S. GILBERT

Anon, Unpacking the Hamper

'Good old Teddie' and Queen Alexandra were not only generous to their employees at Christmas but also admirably imaginative as what each might like. Which other servants in the land received cutlery, and silver at that? Such a gift would be treasured for a lifetime and go on to become a family heirloom. Characteristically, the King and Queen were also providers of some fun for their staff.

Christmas 1902 at Sandringham gave me a glimpse of the thoughtfulness of King Edward and Queen Alexandra on matters affecting their Household staff. There were always big parties at this time of the year, but to compensate for the extra work this entailed the staff were given a Christmas tree in the servants'

at times for those who had families to maintain. Twice a year, therefore, there were presents of a brace of pheasants and a haunch of venison for all servants, and at Christmas there was a joint of beef for all the families on the estate. In addition, the staff Christmas tree was hung with presents of silverware from the King, so that in time each servant could have a full canteen of cutlery. He began the gift in my case with half a dozen forks, the following year I received knives, and so on. They were extremely handsome sets, and were treasured by all the staff.

About that time Queen Alexandra decided that New Year's Eve ought to be celebrated more gaily by the staff, and suggested that a fancy-dress ball should be held. The idea was received enthusiastically, and we set about decorating the servants' hall with paper streamers and preparing spiced old ale made from a Buckingham Palace recipe, which was served with pieces of toast floating in it and at the last moment was stirred with a red-hot poker. There were some very original costumes, particularly amongst some of the footmen, who came dressed as members of a shooting-party, and quite a number of the royal guests came down to watch the proceedings. We did not expect Queen Alexandra, but she arrived shortly before midnight in a magnificent gown of white tulle, looking gay and radiant. She wished us a happy New Year, and from then on always attended the servants' New Year's Eve balls, though we never saw the King on these occasions. ■

GABRIEL TSCHUMT, *ROYAL CHEF*

quarters, and all the members of the royal party contributed gifts to it. The King's gifts were the most magnificent of all. He approved thoroughly of the practice Queen Victoria had introduced of giving the servants something useful at Christmas, for he understood how low royal wages were and how difficult it was

OPPOSITE: *Anon,* Going Down to Christmas Supper

MULLED ALE

2–3 cinnamon sticks
3 blades of mace
4 cloves
1 teaspoon nutmeg
1 pint brown ale
$\frac{1}{2}$ teaspoon of honey
tablespoon of brandy
lemon rind

Heat ale, honey and spices, and leave for thirty minutes. Strain, reheat and pour into warm jug. Add brandy and lemon rind.

NICHOLAS CULPEPER, *HERBAL*

MULLED WINE

Enough for a party of 12.
2 bottles of red wine (if claret more
  sugar should be added)
1 bottle ginger ale
4 cinnamon sticks
Dessert spoon of mixed spice
8 oz / 250 g / 1 cup sugar
An orange stuck with cloves
1 sherry glass of rum, brandy or whisky

Heat all the ingredients in a pan thoroughly, but do not boil. Add glass of spirits before serving.

The setting is Paris and the chief characters a homesick English and Scottish artist in this extract from George du Maurier's popular novel *Trilby*, the story of a young girl hypnotized to stardom by the sinister Svengali. George du Maurier's son, Gerald, became a famous Edwardian actor-manager, and played the original Captain Hook in the first performance of *Peter Pan*.

Roast Fowl.

Pheasant.

Game Pie with Jelly.

Shrimp Patties.

Oyster Patties.

Lobster Salad.

Savoury Jelly à la Bellevue.

Brawn.

Pigeon Pie.

Galantine of Veal.

Russian Salad.

Crayfish.

Ham Garnished.

Tongue Garnished.

CHRISTMAS WAS DRAWING NEAR

There were days when the whole Quartier Latin would veil its iniquities under fogs almost worthy of the Thames Valley between London Bridge and Westminster, and out of the studio window the prospect was a dreary blank ... Taffy and the Laird grew pensive and dreamy, child-like and bland; and when they talked it was generally about Christmas at home in Merry England and the distant Land of Cakes, and how good it was to be there at such a time – hunting, shooting, curling, and endless carouse!

It was Ho! for the jolly West Riding, and Hey! for the bonnets of Bonnie Dundee, till they grew quite homesick, and wanted to start by the very next train.

They didn't do anything so foolish. They wrote over to friends in London for the biggest turkey, the biggest plum pudding, that could be got for love or money, with mincepies, and holly and mistletoe, and sturdy short, thick English sausages; half a Stilton cheese, and a sirloin of beef – two sirloins, in case one should not be enough.

For they meant to have a Homeric feast in the studio on Christmas Day. The cooking and waiting should be done by Trilby, her friend Angèle Boisse, M et Mme Vinard, and such little Vinards as could be trusted with glass and crockery and mincepies; and if that was not enough, they would also cook themselves, and wait upon each other.

When dinner should be over supper was to follow with scarcely any interval to speak of; and to partake of this other guests should be bidden – Svengali and Gecko, and perhaps one or two more ...

Wines and spirits and English beers were procured at great cost from M.E. Delevingne's, in the rue St Honoré, and liqueurs of every description – chartreuse, curacoa, *ratafia de cassis*, and anisette; no expense was spared. ∎

GEORGE DU MAURIER, *TRILBY*

'GRUEL WITH ITS BEST CLOTHES ON' OR 'GRUEL IN A TOP HAT'

Kibbled wheat is simmered in milk in a large pot for anything from 6 to 12 hours. During this time raisins, mixed spice, brown sugar and butter are added. About 15 minutes before serving, cream is stirred in and, just prior to serving, rum or brandy is added. Quantities of ingredients are very much by rule of thumb and to individual taste, but the end result should resemble a thick soup.

Frumenty or furmenty is a traditional 'gruel' well worth sampling. It was eaten on various festive occasions in the past but most particularly on Christmas Eve.

AN ATROCIOUS INSTITUTION

Randolph Caldecott, The Christmas Feast

The acerbic comments of the famous playwright and music-critic George Bernard Shaw offer a Scrooge-like contrast to the abundance of seasonal goodwill. Possibly his being a vegetarian had something to do with his lack of enthusiasm.

The World, 20 December 1893 Like all intelligent people, I greatly dislike Christmas. It revolts me to see a whole nation refrain from music for weeks together in order that every man may rifle his neighbour's pockets under cover of a ghastly general pretence of festivity. It is really an atrocious institution, this Christmas. We must be gluttonous because it is Christmas. We must be drunken because it is Christmas. We must be insincerely generous; we must buy things that nobody wants, and give them to people we don't like; we must go to absurd entertainments that make even our little children satirical; we must writhe under venal officiousness from legions of freebooters, all because it is Christmas – that is, because the mass of the population, including the all-powerful middle-class tradesman, depends on a week of licence and brigandage, waste and intemperance, to clear off its outstanding liabilities at the end of the year.

As for me, I shall fly from it all tomorrow or next day to some remote spot miles from a shop, where nothing worse can befall me than a serenade from a few peasants, or some equally harmless survival of medieval mummery, shyly proffered, not advertised, moderate in its expectations, and soon over. In town there is, for the moment, nothing for me or any honest man to do. ∎

GEORGE BERNARD SHAW

Having read Isabella Beeton's notes on turkeys, what to buy and how to cook it, a young housewife would feel well able to cope with her first Christmas dinner – as well as impress with her knowledge of the festive bird.

ROAST TURKEY

Ingredients: Turkey; forcemeat.

Mode: Having dressed and stuffed the bird, fasten a sheet of buttered paper over the breast, put it down to a bright fire, at some little distance at first (afterwards draw it nearer), and keep it well basted the whole of the time it is cooking. About a quarter of an hour before serving remove the paper, dredge the turkey lightly with flour, and put a piece of butter into the basting-ladle; as the butter melts, baste the bird with it. When of a nice brown and well frothed, serve with a tureen of good brown gravy and bread sauce. Fried sausages are a favourite addition to roast turkey; they make a pretty garnish, besides adding very much to the flavour. When these are not at hand, a few forcemeat balls should be placed round the dish as a garnish. Turkey may also be stuffed with sausagemeat, and a chestnut forcemeat with the sauce is, by many persons, much esteemed as an accompaniment to this favourite dish.

Time: small turkey, $1\frac{1}{2}$ hour; moderate size one, about 10 lbs, 2 hours; large turkey, $2\frac{1}{2}$ hours or longer.

Average cost: from 7*s*. 6.*d* to 10*s*. 6*d*., but expensive at Christmas on account of the great demand.

Sufficient: a moderate-sized turkey, for 7 or 8 persons. Seasonable from December to February.

Note: choose cock turkeys by their short spurs and black legs, in which case they are young; if the spurs are long, and legs pale and rough, they are old. If the bird has been long killed, the eyes will appear sunk and the feet very dry; but, if fresh, the contrary will be the case.

Middling-sized fleshy turkeys are by many persons considered superior to those of an immense growth, as they are, generally speaking, much more tender. They should never be dressed the same day as they are killed; but, in cold weather, should hang at least eight days; if the weather is mild, four or five days will be found sufficient.

English Turkeys: these are reared in great numbers in Suffolk, Norfolk and several other counties, whence they are wont to be driven to the London market in flocks of several hundreds;

the improvements in our modes of travelling now, however, enable them to be brought by railway. Their drivers used to manage them with great facility, by means of a bit of red rag tied to the end of a long stick, which, from the antipathy these birds have to that colour, effectually answered the purpose of a scourge. There are three varieties of the turkey in this country – the black, the white and the speckled or copper-coloured. The black approaches nearest the original stock, and is esteemed the best. Its flesh is white and tender, delicate, nourishing and of excellent flavour; it greatly deteriorates with age, however, and is then good for little but stewing. ∎

The turkey was introduced to this country from North America, and like Father Christmas, also from the New World, came to stay. Originally a wild bird, it was reared from eggs found in the forest or from birds caught when young.

Anon, The Christmas Turkey (card)

CHESTNUT FORCEMEAT

For roast fowl or turkey.

$\frac{1}{2}$ lb / 225 g chestnuts
liver of fowl or turkey
2 oz / 50 g / $\frac{1}{4}$ cup chopped lean ham or bacon
1 oz / 25g / 2 tbsp chopped onion
1 oz / 25 g / 2 tbsp butter
1 egg yolk
2 tbsp stock (from chestnuts or liver)
2 oz / 50 g / 1 cup soft breadcrumbs
1 tsp chopped parsley
$\frac{1}{2}$ tsp salt $\frac{1}{4}$ tsp pepper

Slit the chestnuts, boil or bake for 15 minutes, then peel them. Cook them for 20 minutes in boiling water or stock to cover, then remove them from the pan, pound or mash them in a basin. Finely chop the liver, or mash it with a fork if it is already cooked, and mix it with the chestnuts. Put in the onion, bacon and breadcrumbs, then add the parsley and seasonings. Melt the butter in a small pan, add the egg yolk, and mix with the stock; then use this mixture to bind together the dry ingredients in the basin.

Though written in 1755, Mrs Glasse's recommendations as to the best way to roast a turkey still hold good.

MORE OF THE TURKEY

The best way to roast a Turkey is to loosen the skin on the Breast of the Turkey, and fill it with Force Meat, made thus: Take a Quarter of a Pound of Beef Sewet, as many Crumbs of Bread, a little Lemon peel, an Anchovy, some Nutmeg, Pepper, Parsley and a little Thyme. Chop and beat them all well together, mix them with the Yolk of an Egg, and stuff up the Breast; when you have no Sewet, Butter will do; or you may make your Force Meat thus: Spread Bread and Butter thin, and grate some Nutmeg over it; when you have enough roll it up, and stuff the Breast of the Turkey; then roast it of a fine Brown, but be sure to pin some white Paper [i.e. grease-proof] on the Breast till it is near enough. You must have a good gravy in the Dish, and Bread-Sauce, made thus: Take a good piece of Crumb, put it into a pint of Water, with a blade or two of Mace, two or three Cloves, and some Whole Pepper, Boil it up five or six times, then with a spoon take out the Spice you had before put in, and then you must pour off the Water (you may boil an Onion in it if you please) then beat up the Bread with a good Piece of Butter and a little Salt. ■

MRS GLASSE, *THE ART OF COOKERY MADE PLAIN AND EASY*

Not for many centuries has a boar's head been regarded as customary Christmas fare except at The Queen's College, Oxford, where it is ceremoniously paraded whilst the following carol is sung.

THE BOAR'S HEAD CAROL

The boar's head in hand bear I,
Bedecked with bays and rosemary;
And I pray you, my masters, be merry,
Quot estis in convivio:
Caput apri defero,
Reddens laudes Domino.*

The boar's head, as I understand,
Is the rarest dish in all the land
When thus bedecked with a gay garland,
Let us servire cantico:†

Our steward hath provided this
In honour of the King of bliss,
Which on this day to be served is,
In Reginensi atrio:‡

*Quot, etc. *So many as are in the feast.* Caput, etc. *The boar's head I bring, giving praises to God.*
†Servire, etc. *Let us serve with a song.* ‡In, etc. *In the Queen's hall.*

What could be nicer than a home-cured ham, moist and full of flavour? It makes an ideal companion to what is left of the cold turkey.

Anon, The Boar's Head (*postcard*)

Sandwichmen, carrying advertisement boards strapped like tabards to their back and front, are now strangers to our cities but in Edith's day were numerous and affectionately regarded – even by royalty.

KING AND SANDWICHMEN

At the eleventh annual Christmas dinner to the sandwichmen of London, given by the readers of *Reynold's Newspaper* last evening at the Alexandra Trust, City Road, a letter was read from Sir Dighton Probyn on behalf of the King, in which he said he had his Majesty's command to send £10 towards the expenses, and that he was further to express the King's hope that the men might have a pleasant evening. A letter was also read from the Prince of Wales enclosing £10 towards the fund.

It was decided to send telegrams to both the King and the Prince of Wales thanking them for their kind donations, and wishing them a very happy Christmas. ■

DAILY CHRONICLE, 25 DECEMBER 1905

Anon, Christmas Baskets from the Farm, Filled from Garden, Orchard and Wood (*Advertisements from Christmas hampers, 1911*)

TO CURE BACON OR HAMS IN THE DEVONSHIRE WAY

Ingredients: to every 14 lbs of meat allow 2 oz of saltpetre, 2 oz of salt prunella, 1 lb of common salt. For the pickle, 3 gallons of water, 5 lbs of common salt, 7 lbs of coarse sugar, 3 lbs of bay salt.

Mode: weigh the sides, hams and cheeks, and to every 14 lbs allow the above proportion of saltpetre, salt prunella and common salt. Pound and mix these together, and rub well into the meat; lay it in a stone trough or tub, rubbing it thoroughly, and turning it daily for two successive days. At the end of the second day, pour on it a pickle made as follows; Put the above ingredients into a saucepan, set it on the fire, and stir frequently; remove all the scum, allow it to boil for a quarter of an hour, and pour it hot over the meat. Let the hams be well rubbed and turned daily; if the meat is small, a fortnight will be sufficient for the sides and shoulders to remain in the pickle, and the hams three weeks; if from 30 lbs and upwards, three weeks will be required for the sides etc., and from four to five weeks for the hams. On taking the pieces out, let them drain for an hour, cover with dry sawdust, and smoke from a fortnight to three weeks. Boil and carefully skin the pickle after using, and it will keep good, closely corked for two years. When boiling it for use, add about 2 lbs of common salt and the same of treacle, to allow for waste. Tongues are excellent put into this pickle cold, having been first rubbed with saltpetre and salt and allowed to remain twenty-four hours, not forgetting to make a deep incision under the thick part of the tongue, so as to allow the pickle to penetrate more readily. A fortnight or three weeks, according to the size of the tongue, will be sufficient.

Time: small meat to remain in the pickle a fortnight, hams three weeks; to be smoked from a fortnight to three weeks. ■

MRS BEETON'S *BOOK OF HOUSEHOLD MANAGEMENT*

Family occasions, especially Christmas, are not always as harmonious as expected, various members of the family grating on the nerves of others, but Mr Pooter certainly had no serious complaints to make.

From Punch *1908*

The Christmas Sermon
LITTLE GIRL: '*Daddy, does he know that we dine at one?*'

Christmas Day We caught the 10.20 train at Paddington, and spent a pleasant day at Carrie's mother's. The country was quite nice and pleasant, although the roads were sloppy. We dined in the middle of the day, just ten of us, and talked over old times. If everybody had a nice, *un*interfering mother-in-law, such as I have, what a deal of happiness there would be in the world. Being all in good spirits, I proposed her health; and I made, I think, a very good speech.

I concluded, rather neatly, by saying, 'On an occasion like this – whether relatives, friends, or acquaintances – we are all inspired with good feelings towards each other. 'We are of one mind, and think only of love and friendship. Those who have quarrelled with absent friends should kiss and make up. Those who happily have *not* fallen out, can kiss all the same.'

I saw the tears in the eyes of both Carrie and her mother, and must say I felt very flattered by the compliment. That dear old Reverend John Panzy Smith, who married us, made a most

cheerful and amusing speech, and said he should act on my suggestion respecting the kissing. He then walked round the table and kissed all the ladies, including Carrie. Of course one did not object to this: but I was more than staggered when a young fellow named Moss, who was a stranger to me, and who had scarcely spoken a word through dinner, jumped up suddenly with a sprig of mistletoe, and exclaimed, 'Hulloh! I don't see why I shouldn't be in on this scene.' Before one could realize what he was about to do, he kissed Carrie and the rest of the ladies.

Fortunately the matter was treated as a joke, and we all laughed; but it was a dangerous experiment, and I felt very uneasy for a moment as to the result. I subsequently referred to the matter to Carrie, but she said, 'Oh, he's not much more than a boy.' I said that he had a very large moustache for a boy. Carrie replied, 'I didn't say he was not a nice boy.' ■

GEORGE AND WEEDON GROSSMITH, *DIARY OF A NOBODY*

Decorated with holly and illumined by flaming brandy, Christmas pudding, is the crowning glory of the feast. Important tip: warm the brandy in a ladle before pouring it over the pudding and setting it alight. It is prepared on the last Sunday before Advent. Stir-up Sunday is when each member of the household takes a turn to stir in an anti-clockwise direction, the mixture before it is cooked. A ritual fondly remembered by Elizabeth Yandell in her book *Henry*. 'Authority' who donated the threepenny bits, is her father and Henry, the gardener, her chief companion.

Anon, Stirring the Pudding

Cookie's word was law . . . In a house without a mistress to boss her around, she ruled supreme and supremely well. We lacked nothing she could provide for us, nor did anyone who came to us in need or trouble. She made Christmas puddings by the dozen, one for each household on the estate and quite a few spares which Dr Harris collected for his very poor patients. They were round puddings, boiled in linen clothes – no basins – in the big clothes coppers in the laundry . . .

There were jobs for everybody. I always helped with raisins, big plummy ones, and they had to be stoned. '*Only* the stones, mind, not the flesh!' Preparing the fruit was a military operation at the end of every September. Mrs Dence and Mrs Havinden came in to do the currants and sultanas. First they were all washed – and they came in twenty-eight-pound bags, jute bags,

of ale. All this was mixed, covered with the trough lid, and left to ripen the flavours. Next afternoon the boilers were filled and the fires lit. The ironing table was covered with the pudding cloths ready scaled and floured. It was a time of celebration.

Cookie added the requisite quantity of flour and fine bread-crumbs and, with sleeves rolled up almost to her shoulders, plunged both hands into the mixture and pummelled away until she was satisfied that it was mixed. This was the great moment. All in the house gathered for the ceremonial adding of the luck. Authority was first; into the mixture he emptied a bank bag of threepenny bits and took a stir. One after the other we all followed. It was such fun.

Most of us lingered until Cookie had given the whole mass a distributing turnover, doled out the mixture into the cloths

hairy and sticky . . .

Liz did the candied peel, gorgeous stuff. Halves of orange and lemon peels, each with a lovely lump of candy sugar in the hollows. Cookie did all the suet herself, to be certain that no bits of fleshy, gristly skin slipped in to vex the teeth at table . . .

In the laundry a great wooden bread trough was set up on trestles beside the ironing table. Into the trough went all the ingredients as they were ready. Nutmeg, spices, almonds and sugar were added, together with a bottle of brandy and a quart

and the first batch of puds was merrily boiling. Henry and Jack sat up long after the rest of us were in bed. Those puds had to boil for eight hours. When done they were lifted out on to sieves and when they were cold each was brushed with brandy a new cloth covering added. They kept wonderfully.

The stirring ceremony seemed to me, even when I was very small, to be something very special, something that preserved a bond between us all. ■

ELIZABETH YANDELL, *HENRY*

Christmas pudding, often called plum pudding because the essential ingredients, dried fruit, were known as plums, was introduced to this country by George I in the eighteenth century.

Boxing Day dates from the Middle Ages when the contents of the church alms boxes, especially put out for the purpose at this time, were distributed amongst the needy. Apprentices also traditionally received small amounts of money from their employers and customers over the year. This would be collected in small earthenware money boxes that would be broken open with anticipation on Boxing Day. In Edith's day it was those who offered a regular service, such as the postman, who would be rewarded, along with the farm labourers and needy cottagers living on the estate of a kindly benefactor.

'Authority' was obviously just such a benefactor.

Authority's Christmas box went to each home along with the pudding. A hamper filled, according to the number in the family, with a piece of beef, a cock pheasant, and a bottle of port, with a cake and two hundredweight of best coals. To this Cookie added a pound of tea, nuts and oranges and a box of crackers. Logs were free for the cutting in coppices. All this was not a charitable handout, nor was it received as such. It was a Christmas gift in goodwill to all. Throughout the length and breadth of England the old landed families did the same ∎

ELIZABETH YANDELL, *HENRY*

Charles Hunt, High Life Below Stairs

CHRISTMAS PLUM-PUDDING
(*Very Good*)

Ingredients: $1\frac{1}{2}$ lb. of raisins, $\frac{1}{2}$ lb. of currants, $\frac{1}{2}$ lb. of mixed peel, $\frac{3}{4}$ lb. bread-crumbs, $\frac{3}{4}$ lb. of suet, 8 eggs, 1 wineglassful of brandy.

Mode: stone and cut the raisins in halves, but do not chop them; wash, pick, and dry the currants, and mince the suet finely; cut the candied peel into thin slices, and grate down the bread into fine crumbs. When all these dry ingredients are prepared, mix them well together; then moisten the mixture with the eggs, which should be well beaten, and the brandy; stir well, that everything may be very thoroughly blended, and *press* the pudding into a buttered mould; tie it down tightly with a floured cloth, and boil for 5 or 6 hours. It may be boiled in a cloth without a mould, and will require the same time allowed for cooking. As Christmas puddings are usually made a few days before they are required for table, when the pudding is taken out of the pot, hang it up immediately and put a plate or saucer underneath to catch the water that may drain from it. The day it is to be eaten, plunge it into boiling water, and keep it boiling for at least two hours; then turn it out of the mould, and serve with brandy-sauce. On Christmas Day a sprig of holly is usually placed in the middle of the pudding, and about a wineglassful of brandy poured round it, which, at the moment of serving, is lighted, and the pudding thus brought to table encircled in flame.

Time: 5 or 6 hours the first time of boiling; 2 hours the day it is to be served.

Average Cost: 3*s.* 3*d.*

Sufficient: for a quart mould for 7 or 8 persons.

Seasonable: on the 25th of December, and on various festive occasions till March.

Note: five or six of these puddings should be made at one time, as they will keep good for many weeks, and in cases where unexpected guests arrive, will be found an acceptable, and, as it only requires warming through, a quickly-prepared dish. Moulds of every shape and size are manufactured for these puddings, and thus a pleasant variety can be made.

MRS BEETON, *BOOK OF HOUSEHOLD MANAGEMENT*

Was this letter to Mr Punch a vehicle to warn readers of the make-up of celluloid, or is there a moral to the tale? Whatever, like all good Christmas stories, it has a happy ending.

OUR CHRISTMAS PUDDING

Dear Mr Punch, I have been reading your tragi-comedy about the charms in the plum pudding and feel particularly sympathetic because something of the same kind very nearly wrecked my own happiness on Christmas day ... It happened like this. We had just arrived at the pudding stage, and I felt it was the moment of my life, and Lizzie, our maid, felt it was the moment of hers, as she bore it to the table in triumph. I could see she'd been having a grim struggle in getting it out of the saucepan, for her face was post-office red, and she had forgotten to turn her sleeves down ...

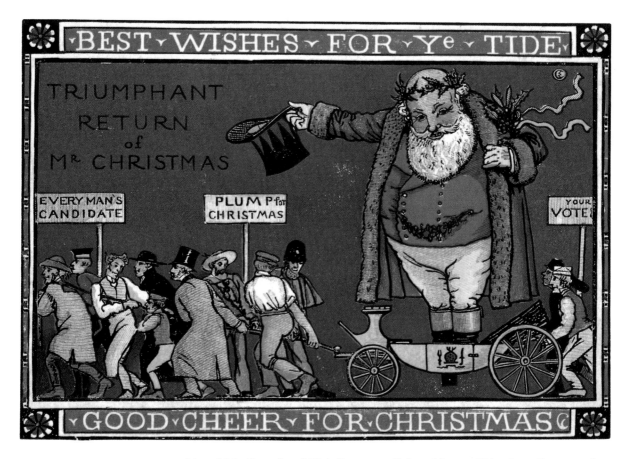

Mr and Mrs Bostock and Dick Barry were dining with us ... and I particularly wanted him to see how domesticated I was, because – well, every woman will know why. The pudding certainly looked a picture, its rich brown complexion showing a vivid contrast to the red holly berries that crowned it, and in

Walter Crane, Christmas card

its firm yet spongy interior I had hidden the usual mascots – a threepenny-bit for riches, a wedding ring for marriage, and a thimble for spinsterhood. I managed to give Mr Bostock the slice with the threepenny-bit in it, and he was delighted at the attainment of more riches; but at the second mouthful I noticed a queer expression cross his face, as he helped himself again to brandy sauce and passed it significantly across to his wife. An eloquent silence fell upon us, till my brother Harry began talking eagerly about the Budget; but even if I had been interested I couldn't have joined in, for I was too occupied with wondering what it could be that made the pudding taste of camphor . . . Mrs Bostock gave a startled ejaculation and stared at something on her plate. Everybody stopped eating with wonderful willingness.

'What is it, Mrs Bostock?' I exclaimed.

'*You* ought to know that best,' said Harry, hooking up the offending object on his fork. It was a soft, whitish thing, and looked like a flabby capsule of sodden paper.

'Why, it's *only* the thimble,' I exclaimed, much relieved.

'The thimble!' they all cried, incredulously.

'Yes,' I replied. 'I couldn't find my silver one, so I put in Lizzie's. It was made of celluloid, and I expect the – the *goodness* has all boiled out of it.'

'Good heavens! We're poisoned,' groaned Mrs Bostock.

Harry turned on me with a face like a thunder-cloud.

'You must be *mad*,' he said. 'I thought you had more sense. No wonder the beastly stuff tasted of camphor.'

'*Camphor*, indeed!' exclaimed Mr Bostock. 'Do you know, young lady, that celluloid contains nitric and sulphuric acid and chloride of lime?'

I shook my head. If I'd tried to speak I should have burst out crying. As it was, my eyes were full of tears.

'All excellent things for the system when taken in small quantities,' said Dick Barry. 'It's the best pudding I've ever tasted, Miss Mabel. May I have some more, please?'

And, in spite of all they could say to dissuade him he had another slice . . . and got the wedding ring; and when, after the Bostocks had gone, and we had been engaged about seven minutes, he asked Harry if he would trust my life to him, Harry replied, 'Certainly, if you'll trust yours to her.' Which showed that the nitric acid and chloride of lime were still rankling.

Yours sincerely, Mabel Green. ■

PUNCH, JANUARY 1909

We may live without friends, we may live without books, but civilized man cannot live without cooks.
EDWARD ROBERT
BULWER-LYTTON

After a good dinner, one can forgive anybody even one's own relations.
OSCAR WILDE

The cook was a good cook, as cooks go: and as cooks go she went.
SAKI (H.H. MUNRO)

Originally the mince pie was made in the shape of the cradle, oblong and decorated with a child made of pastry, but the Commonwealth year saw the end of this custom, and when they returned once more they were circular. It is believed by many that if a mince pie is eaten on each of the twelve days of Christmas, twelve happy months will follow. Most consider this no great hardship.

FRUIT IN BRANDY

This is an old way of keeping the very best fruit for a special occasion, such as Christmas, when it can be served in glass dishes with cream or ice-cream and small sponge cakes or shortbread biscuits. Follow the first 1 lb/450 g fruit and sugar with different fruits as they come into season: strawberries, loganberries, apricots, cherries and plums can be used.

1 lb/450 g ripe strawberries
1 lb/450 g lump or granulated sugar
1 bottle good brandy

Use a large jar such as a sweet jar or a stoneware pot, with a tight-fitting lid; make sure it is perfectly clean and dry. Small whole strawberries are best but larger ones quartered can be used; place them in the bottom of the jar, cover with the sugar and pour in the brandy. Seal well, with a layer of greaseproof or brown paper tied over the lid. When the next fruit, with the same amount of sugar, is added, stir the contents of the jar first, then put in fruit and sugar as before. Do this with each addition of fruit and sugar – up to 5 lb/2$\frac{1}{2}$ kg can be preserved to each bottle of brandy.

MINCEMEAT

The meat which was traditionally used to make mincemeat has long since been replaced by suet, but sometimes even this is thought to be too rich. Here is an old recipe which omits it altogether; if you wish to include it, add $\frac{1}{2}$ lb/225 g lb shredded suet but remember that alcohol is needed if mincemeat is to be kept any length of time – a wine glass of brandy can also be added.

$\frac{1}{2}$ lb/225 g/1$\frac{1}{4}$ cups raisins
$\frac{1}{2}$ lb/225 g/1$\frac{1}{3}$ cups currants
$\frac{1}{2}$ lb/225 g/2 cups sultanas
$\frac{1}{2}$ lb/225 g/1 cup soft brown or demerara sugar
$\frac{1}{4}$ lb/125 g/$\frac{2}{3}$ cup chopped candied peel
1$\frac{1}{2}$ lb/675 g apples
1 lemon
1 nutmeg

Stone and chop the raisins and mix them with the other dried fruit and the peel. Peel, core and mince or finely chop the apples; mix them with the fruit. Add the grated rind and the juice of the lemon and the finely grated nutmeg; stir very well and leave to stand in the bowl overnight. If using suet mix this in at the same time as the dried fruit; sprinkle the brandy over with the lemon juice. Next day stir well, put it in dry jars, and cover with greaseproof paper.

The memory of the miserable Christmas Day suffered by Edmund Gosse during his childhood did not leave him and one wonders whether, in consequence, he allowed his own children to indulge fully in all the fun and festivity of the season. The extract is taken from what is considered his masterpiece, *Father and Son*, which he described as 'the record of a struggle between two temperaments, two consciences and almost two epochs'.

BRANDY BUTTER

This is traditionally served, either with or without custard sauce, with plum pudding at Christmas.

4 oz / 125 g / 1 stick butter
3 oz / 75 g / ¾ cup caster sugar (fine sugar)
2–3 tbsp brandy

Cream the butter and sugar together until very soft. Beat in the brandy a little at a time so that the mixture is light and smooth; serve chilled in a glass dish. Rum butter is made in the same way, but soft brown sugar is used instead of white sugar; add ½ tsp of lemon juice if liked.

On the subject of all feasts of the Church he [Father] held views of an almost grotesque peculiarity. He looked upon each of them as nugatory and worthless, but the keeping of Christmas appeared to him by far the most hateful, and nothing less than an act of idolatry. 'The very word is Popish,' he used to exclaim, 'Christ's Mass!' pursing up his lips with the gesture of one who tastes assafoetida by accident. Then he would adduce the antiquity of the so-called feast, adapted from horrible heathen rites, and itself a soiled relic of the abominable Yule-Tide. He would denounce the horrors of Christmas until it almost made me blush to look at a holly-berry.

On Christmas Day of this year 1857 our villa saw a very unusual sight. My Father had given strictest charge that no difference whatever was to be made in our meals on that day; the dinner was to be neither more copious than usual nor less so. He was obeyed, but the servants, secretly rebellious, made a small plum pudding for themselves. (I discovered afterwards, with pain, that Miss Marks received a slice of it in her boudoir.) Early in the afternoon, the maids – of whom we were now advanced to keeping two – kindly remarked that 'the poor dear child ought to have a bit, anyhow', and wheedled me into the kitchen, where I ate a slice of plum pudding. Shortly I began to feel that pain inside which in my frail state was inevitable, and my conscience smote me violently. At length I could bear my spiritual anguish no longer, and bursting into the study I called out, 'Oh! Papa, Papa, I have eaten of flesh offered to idols!' It took some time, between my sobs, to explain what had happened. Then my Father sternly said, 'Where is the accursed thing?' I explained that as much as was left of it was still on the kitchen table. He took me by the hand, and ran with me into the midst of the startled servants, seized what remained of the pudding, and with the plate in one hand and me still tight in the other, ran till we reached the dust-heap, when he flung the idolatrous confectionery on to the middle of the ashes, and then raked it deep down into the mass. The suddenness, the violence, the velocity of this extraordinary act made an impression on my memory which nothing will ever efface. ■

EDMUND GOSSE, *FATHER AND SON*

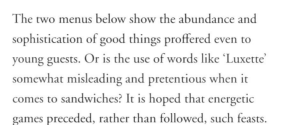

The two menus below show the abundance and sophistication of good things proffered even to young guests. Or is the use of words like 'Luxette' somewhat misleading and pretentious when it comes to sandwiches? It is hoped that energetic games preceded, rather than followed, such feasts.

A CHRISTMAS WEDDING

The first girl lived in a country town and evergreens in the woods near by were plentiful. The wedding was a Christmas one, and took place in the late afternoon. Garlands of graceful ground pine were wound over the banisters in the hall, and draped over the doorways to hang down halfway on each side against the ivory white woodwork. In the living-room, two little Christmas trees, lighted with tiny white candles, formed an alcove where the bridal group could stand.

The table in the dining-room was decorated for a buffet luncheon in holiday red and green. There was a centrepiece of red roses, red silk candle shades shading white candles in clear glass candlesticks, and tiny green Christmas ferns scattered on the white cloth.

The menu had the same colour harmony, and consisted of consommé, salted crackers, oyster patties, chicken jelly salad with green mayonnaise, salad rolls, olives, pistachio ice-cream in holly-decked cases, little cakes with green icing and silver bonbons stuck on top, and coffee, with green mints.

EMILY ROSE BURT, *ENTERTAINING MADE EASY*

The description of a Christmas wedding attended by Emily Rose Burt might well have inspired other young couples to marry at this time of year, as well as given hostesses some ideas on Christmas party food and decorations.

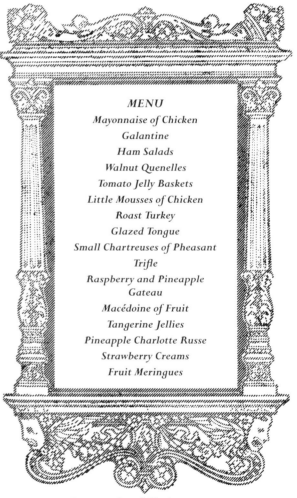

MENU
Mayonnaise of Chicken

Galantine

Ham Salads

Walnut Quenelles

Tomato Jelly Baskets

Little Mousses of Chicken

Roast Turkey

Glazed Tongue

Small Chartreuses of Pheasant

Trifle

Raspberry and Pineapple Gateau

Macédoine of Fruit

Tangerine Jellies

Pineapple Charlotte Russe

Strawberry Creams

Fruit Meringues

Suggestions for a children's supper party

And then, after the Christmas lunch, there is tea, and how can one resist a slice, albeit wafer thin, of the Christmas cake encased in its thick coat of marzipan and icing.

PLUM CAKE

A rich, dark cake, this can be made using double quantities for Christmas.

$\frac{1}{2}$ lb / 225 g / 2 cups flour
6 oz / 175 g / 1$\frac{1}{2}$ sticks butter or margarine
6 oz / 75 g / $\frac{3}{4}$ cup chopped almonds
2 oz / 50 g / 3 tbsp treacle
4 oz / 125 g / $\frac{2}{3}$ cup chopped candied peel
4 oz / 125 g / $\frac{2}{3}$ cup currants
8 oz / 225 g / 1$\frac{1}{4}$ cups raisins
3 eggs
$\frac{1}{4}$ tsp bicarbonate of soda (baking soda)
a little milk if necessary

Grease and line a deep cake tin. Cream the sugar and butter; beat in the eggs, one at a time. Sift in the flour and bicarbonate of soda. Warm the treacle a little, and stir it in, then add the fruit, peel and almonds; add milk if needed to give a stiff but not dry consistency. Bake in a very moderate oven (325°F/160°C/Mark 3) for 2$\frac{1}{2}$–3 hours; put a piece of brown paper over the top for the last hour of cooking if it seems to be browning too quickly.

MENU

Turkey Bouchées

Aspic Nests

Chicken and Ham Cutlets
(Chaudfroid)

Little Russian Salads

Bombs of Tongue

Chicken and Tomato Sandwiches

Luxette Cream Sandwiches

Egg, Cream and Cucumber
Sandwiches

Mayonnaise Sandwiches

Tangerine Baskets

Peaches in Jelly

Trifle

Fruit Salad

Meringues

Petits Fours. Bon-bons

A buffet supper for a juvenile party

THE LADIES' FIELD, CHRISTMAS 1913

And for those who have over-indulged, lessons are learned and help is at hand.

THE RECKONING

Now the festive season's ended,
Comes the sequel parents dread;
Pale and visibly distended
Bilious Tommy lies in bed,
Face to face with retribution
And an outraged constitution.

What a change since, pink and perky,
Tommy swiftly put away
Three enormous goes of turkey
At the feast on Christmas Day,
Getting by judicious bluffing
Double quantities of stuffing.

As to pudding, who could reckon
Tommy's load in terms of size?
Who attempt to keep a check on
Tommy's numberless mince pies?
Hopeless task! His present pallor
Proves his prodigies of valour.

Then I found him, notwithstanding
Such colossal feats as these,
After dinner on the landing
Secretly devouring cheese,
Flanked by ginger-beer-and-coffee,
Sweetened with a slab of toffee.

I, his uncle, gave him warning,
Showed the error of his ways,
Hinted at to-morrow morning,
Talked about my boyhood's days;
All in vain I waved the bogey –
He despised me as a fogey.

Well, perhaps the pains he suffers
May be gifts of fairy gold,
Since he now says, 'Only duffers
Eat as much as they can hold.'
Thus, through physic and privations,
Tommy learns his limitations.

PUNCH, 2 JANUARY 1907

Anon, Traditional Food (*postcard*)

A bowl of glistening crystallized fruits not only looks attractive on the Christmas dinner table, but also proves irresistible. The following is from an Edwardian cookery booklet, *Prize Recipes*. For those who have a greengage, pear, plum, or apricot tree in their garden, making a gift box of home-crystallized fruits could prove the perfect, economical answer to the problem of what to give Uncle Henry.

The fruits must be firm and not too ripe. Remove the skins, and cut any fruit containing stones in half and remove the stones, pare and remove stalks from small pears. Roll the fruit in caster sugar that contains a small saltspoonful each of cream of tartar and bicarbonate of soda to every pound. Pack separately on a dish and cover with sugar. Bake in a hot oven until fruit is tender; remove the dish, stand it in a cool larder, and before the fruit is set cold roll in the sugar mixture again and stand on a wire rack for 24 hours, then place in a box or tin with greaseproof paper between the layers. ∎

PRIZE RECIPES

GIFTS WITH HERBS

Culinary herbs, vinegars, jellies, bouquet garni, fines herbes, *herbal butters and marinades.*

The following collection of edibles made with herbs make excellent
standbys for the cook as well as acceptable gifts.

The use of fresh and dried herbs in cookery is now quite widespread. The lady of the house might no longer have a still room in which to concoct special brews and sweetmeats but her kitchen shelves invariably boast a collection of herbs, and one or two different oils, vinegars or conserves. Here are some variations on some of the herbs, vinegars and conserves that can be stored and used at will to enhance the flavour of a dish or add that extra dash of interest.

Herb vinegars are superb for adding a piquancy to a sauce, relish or stew, salad dressing or marinade. They are easy to make and keep well.

HERB VINEGAR

Pour 1pt (600ml/2½ cups) of cider or white wine vinegar over 6tbs of lightly chopped or crushed herbs such as rosemary, French tarragon, thyme, marjoram, basil, sage or mint. Mustard seeds, chillis and peppercorns can be added according to taste. Cover and leave to steep for a few weeks, then strain. Boil the vinegar and then bottle, adding a fresh sprig of the herb used before sealing with a non-metallic stopper.

HERB BUTTER

Neat pats of herb butter melting on a portion of grilled meat or fish look as good as they taste and are easily made in quantity and stored in the freezer until needed. They can also be served with hot rolls or French bread. Various herbs can be used and the proportions should be as follows: to every 8oz (250g/2½cups)

of butter add 4tbs (heaped) of the chopped herb, salt and pepper, the juice of a lemon or 3 large cloves of garlic.

GARLIC

Garlic goes best with red meat and the herbs rosemary, sage, chervil and marjoram, while the butter containing the grated rind and juice of a lemon goes best with fish, vegetables and white meat and the herbs tarragon, parsley, fennel or lemon thyme.

BOUQUET GARNI

A bouquet garni is a bunch of fresh sprigs of mixed herbs or a small sachet containing dried herbs. The latter is easier to use in soups and stews as it does not break up and can be removed with ease when the cooking process is over. The traditional ingredients are 2 sprigs of parsley, 1 bay leaf and 1 sprig of tarragon. Other herbs such as garlic, celery or fennel can be added, depending on whether the dish is meat- or fish-based.

FINES HERBES

Fines herbes are a mix of the dried or fresh leaves only of 2 parts parsley, 1 of chives and chervil and ½ of tarragon. Always acceptable presents to any keen cook, the little muslin sachets or bags of bouquet garni or *fines herbes* can be wrapped in attractive green- or red-checked cotton and tied with coloured thread.

HERB JELLY

The following herb jelly is an excellent accompaniment to hot or cold ham, chicken, duck, pork or lamb.

Apples
Water
Malt vinegar
Fresh herb
Sugar

Coarsely cut up the apples without peeling or coring them and discard any rotten bits. Place in a pan and cover with water and vinegar: use ¼pt (140ml/½ cup) of vinegar to every 1pt (600ml/2½ cups) of water. Add a good handful of sprigs of one herb, either parsley, thyme, sage or mint, and simmer with the apples until they have been reduced to a pulp. Ladle the contents of the pan into a jelly bag and strain. Measure the strained juice into a preserving pan and to every 1pt (600ml/2½ cups) of liquid add 1lb (450g) of preserving or granulated sugar. Dissolve the sugar in the liquid over a low heat, then bring to the boil and cook until setting point has been reached. Skim any froth from the surface, allow to cool for a few minutes, and to every 1lb (450g) of apples used stir in 1tbs of the chopped herb. Pour into warmed jam jars and cover. ∎

CHRISTMAS ENTERTAINING

The ideal white Christmas seems to have deserted our shores (although prophecy would be rash), and more and more English people flee to Switzerland for the winter sports the clerk of the weather will not let them enjoy at home. There, among the snows, they find a real old-fashioned Christmas, with all the ancient amusements and many new ones. Tobogganing, ski-ing and skating are supplemented by games on the ice. Even cricket has been found possible on skates.

ILLUSTRATED LONDON NEWS,
15 DECEMBER 1906

According to the newspapers, the snow that Christmas came as a surprise to all and lingered in parts of Britain up to the New Year and later. A white Christmas! What a thrill and an opportunity for enthusiasts of all ages to hunt out the skates and toboggan, catch Uncle Freddie unawares with a snowball and make the biggest snowman ever! It was bad luck for those who had decided to spend Christmas – at large expense – at one of the increasingly popular winter sports resorts in Switzerland or Austria to try out that new fad ski-ing when so much fun could be had at home? And when the gloves, boots and hats had become too cold and sodden for comfort and the light dimmed there was always the warm fire inside to curl up in front of. With luck there would still be energy enough to gather round the piano for a few songs or enjoy a hilarious round of charades – a great favourite, especially when friends had been invited around for the evening. Mother might have arranged a party for the children and even gone so far as to have booked a conjuror.

From Boxing Day on there was the exciting prospect of the family outing to the pantomime to look forward to. Which one to go to posed quite a problem as there were so many to choose from. The detailed reviews in all the newspapers made each sound more lavish and fantastic than the last. The Edwardian Christmas was far from dull, especially if it snowed, and it was not so much a matter of *what* to do, but would there be time.

Dec. 28. **Bright and clear, more heavy snow storms are reported from all parts of the country accompanied in some places by thunder and lightning. Skating has commenced in the fens.**

COUNTRY DIARY

116

The Girl's Home Companion gives advice on learning how to skate, but none on first finding a friend.

Robert Barnes, Merry-go-round on the Ice

If you have a friend who can skate, get him to take you into the middle of the ice. The best way is to place both feet together and get him to push you gently along without your attempting to move either foot. This will also give you confidence in the supporting power of your skates. Should you feel yourself falling, do not attempt to save yourself, but drop down gently. Struggling is quite useless, and it is much better to sink down gently without a struggle than to fall heavily in consequence of it . . .
THE GIRL'S HOME COMPANION

Not all achieve this with grace as, the Revd Kilvert commented:

27 December 1870 After dinner drove into Chippenham with Perch and bought two pair of skates at Benk's for 17/6. Across the fields to the Draycot water and the young Awdry ladies chaffed me about my new skates. I had not been on skates since I was here last, five years ago, and was very awkward for the first ten minutes, but the knack soon came again. There was a distinguished company on the ice, Lady Dangan, Lord and Lady Royston and Lord George Paget all skating. Also Lord and Lady Sydney and a Mr Calcroft . . . I had the honour of being knocked down by Lord Royston, who was coming round suddenly on the outside edge... Harriet Awdry skated beautifully and jumped over a half-sunken punt. Arthur Law skating jumped over a chair on its legs.

Thursday, 29 December 1870 Skating at Draycot again with Perch. Fewer people on the ice today. No quadrille band, torches or fireworks, but it was very pleasant, cosy and sociable. Yesterday when the Lancers was being skated Lord Royston was directing the figures . . .

Lady Royston skates very nicely and seems very nice. A sledge chair was put on the ice and Lady Royston and Lady Dangan, Margaret, Fanny, Maria, and Harriet Awdry were drawn about in it by turns, Charles Awdry pushing behind and Edmund and Arthur and Walter pulling with ropes. It was a capital team and went at a tremendous pace up and down the ice. A German ladies' maid from Draycot House was skating and making ridiculous antics.

New Year's Day, 1871 When Perch came back from skating at Draycot last night, he amused us with an account of Friday's and Saturday's doings on the ice. On Friday they had a quadrille band from Malmesbury, skated quadrilles, Lancers, and Sir Roger de Coverley. Then they skated up and down with torches, ladies and gentlemen pairing off and skating arm in arm, each with a torch. There were numbers of Chinese lanterns all round the water, blue, crimson and green lights, magnesium riband, and a fire balloon was sent up. ■

FRANCIS KILVERT, *DIARY 1870–79*

It was not only the children who revelled in the ice and snow, but also the young ladies and gentlemen of the day. Such pursuits gave them an opportunity to meet informally and show off their grace on the ice – if they had been fortunate enough to acquire it.

L. Prang & Co (after a work by Henry Sandham), Skating

AN IDYL ON THE ICE

Fur-apparelled for the skating,
Comes the pond's acknowledged Belle;
I am duly there in waiting,
For I'll lose no time in stating
That I love the lady well.

Then to don her skates, and surely
Mine the task to fit them tight,
Strap and fasten them securely
While she offers me, demurely,
First the left foot then the right.

Off she circles, swiftly flying
To the pond's extremest verge;
Then returning, and replying
With disdain to all my sighing,
And the love I dare not urge.

Vainly do I follow after,
She's surrounded in a trice,
Other men have come and chaffed her,
And the echo of her laughter
Comes across the ringing ice.

Still I've hope, a hope that never
In my patient heart is dead;
Though fate for a time might sever,
Though she skated on for ever,
I would follow where she fled.
        MR PUNCH'S BOOK OF SPORTS

Christmas Eve 1874 Speaking of people slipping and falling
on ice the good churchwarden sagely remarked, 'Some do fall
on their faces and some do fall on their rumps. And they as do
hold their selves uncommon stiff do most in generally fall on
their rumps.' ∎

        FRANCIS KILVERT, *DIARY 1870–79*

from SKATING

And in the frosty season, when the sun
Was set, and visible for many a mile
The cottage windows blazed through
*   twilight gloom,*
I heeded not their summons: happy time
It was indeed for all of us – for me
It was a time of rapture! Clear and loud
The village clock tolled six, – I wheeled about,
Proud and exulting like an untired horse
That cares not for his home. All shod with steel,
We hissed along the polished ice in games
Confederate, imitative of the chase
And woodland pleasures, – the resounding horn,
The pack loud chiming, and the hunted hare.
So through the darkness and the cold we flew,
And not a voice was idle; with the din
Smitten, the precipices rang aloud;
The leafless trees and every icy crag
Tinkled like iron; while far distant hills
Into the tumult sent an alien sound
Of melancholy not unnoticed, while the stars
Eastward were sparkling clear . . .

WILLIAM WORDSWORTH

The still beauty of the frozen scene and the various noises that floated across the expanse of ice caught Wordsworth's imagination.

Advice was on offer for the Edwardian child as well as adult on every aspect of life, even what games to play in the snow.

SNOW GAMES

It is very easy for boys and girls to invent snow games for themselves; but a few hints as to how to set about it may be useful.

First and foremost it should be remembered that snowballs should not be weighted with stones or heavy substances, which render them dangerous missiles instead of harmless and amusing ones.

Freshly fallen snow should be chosen, and before the game commences, the players should be divided into sides and each side should employ all its members to make snowballs as fast as they can. It is very unfair for the elder members to set the little ones to this work, whilst they are enjoying the fun of aiming the balls.

The side which works the quickest naturally has the largest supply of ammunition and stands a better chance of winning.

HAMPSTEAD GOES TOBOGGANING

The best toboggan ground around London is Parliament Hill, the top of which is four hundred feet above sea level. At least 5000 persons were on the hill every afternoon, and the fun was kept up by the moonlight until quite a late hour.

ILLUSTRATED LONDON NEWS, 5 JANUARY 1906

L. Prang & Co (after a work by Henry Sandham), Tobogganing

large snow balls, rolling them about in the snow until they are about a foot in height and then placing them side by side to form a square. On these pile others until a wall of balls is formed; the spaces between the balls must be filled in with snow, and a doorway must be left for the besieged party to sally forth from, when more snow for ammunition is required.

The besieged must remember the besiegers have any amount of snow handy, whereas their own stock is, of necessity, limited, and they must take care to have as large a number of balls ready as possible.

When the castle is completed, the ammunition stocked, and the besiegers likewise provided with a good supply of balls, at a given signal the battle commences. ∎

THE GAMES BOOK FOR BOYS AND GIRLS

Lines should be drawn between which the combatants stand to fight, and whichever side drives the other side over the line is counted victor.

Another very good snow game is to build a fort, or snow castle, but this takes some time to prepare.

The best method is to make a number of very

SCHOOLBOYS IN WINTER

The schoolboys still their morning rambles take
To neighbouring village school with playing speed,
Loitering with pastime's leisure till they quake,
Oft looking up the wild-geese droves to heed,
Watching the letters which their journeys make;
Or plucking haws on which the fieldfares feed
And hips, and sloes; and on each shallow lake
Making glib slides, where they like shadows go
Till some fresh pastimes in their minds awake.
Then off they start anew and hasty blow
Their numbed and clumpsing fingers till they glow;
Then races with their shadows wildly run
That stride huge giants o'er the shining snow
In the pale splendour of the winter sun.

JOHN CLARE

A Merry Christmas

To good little girls and good little boys
May Christmas bring you lots of joys

Cycling was all the rage in Edith's day and played a liberating role in many women's lives. If the Christmas was not a white one, a cycle ride was as good a way to shake down the Christmas pudding as skating or tobogganing. But the young lady was urged to take certain precautions.

Do not ride unattended by a male relative or friend. Do not accompany club runs unless specially small and select. Always ride in correct cycling costume. Stick to the 'all-wool' principle, and do not have your skirt either too long or too full, these being fertile sources of accident. Do not lace tightly. Use a saddle, not a seat, and preferably a saddle with a short neck, as specially constructed for ladies' use; a back may be used if preferred. When touring, carry your own soap, also a box of Brand's or Johnston's meat lozenges, and a few tablets of chocolate or good Muscatel raisins. These by way of roadside 'pick-me-ups'. Carry a waterproof cape, *but do not ride in it*. Carry a menthol cone. Drawn gently over the forehead, it is a capital thing for headache, or to soothe the nerves when over-fatigue will not let you sleep. ■

GIRL'S HOME COMPANION

John Morgan, A Winter Landscape with Boys Snowballing

Cycled to Solihull, and back through
the lanes past the oak woods. The sun
was shining brightly; lighting up the
dying fronds of Bracken among the
under-growth, and the scanty
foliage on the half bare Oak trees.
The leaves lay thick all along the way.
I heard a Thrush singing most
sweetly in the big Beech tree at the
top of Kineton Lane.

COUNTRY DIARY

CHRISTMAS PARTIES

In Edwardian times, children's parties were
elaborate affairs and endless advice was on
offer as to what games to play and what to eat.
Along with old familiars like 'Blind Man's
Buff' and 'Oranges and Lemons', 'Dumb
Crambo' was a favourite. The American writer
Mrs Herbert B. Linscott was never short of a
good idea, many of which must have been
highly popular, involving as they did, the
receiving of a gift. They also involved a
considerable amount of effort and expense for
the parents.

Albert Chevallier Taylor, The Christmas Tree

CHILDREN'S CHRISTMAS PARTY

There in the library stood the most perfect snowman. He wore a fur cap and long white whiskers, and on the floor behind him lay his pack, which had just slipped off his back. He held a doll on one arm, and over the other was hung a line of tiny sleigh-bells. This snow Santa Claus was made of cotton batting, but he looked exactly like the snow-man in the yard, and the children greeted him with cries of delight.

Each child was allowed to throw a soft rubber ball twice in attempting to hit the string of bells which Santa held. Those who were successful were told to take some article out of the pack as a reward. Fancy cornucopias and small boxes filled with nuts and candy were found by the lucky contestants.

Then came old-fashioned romping games, after which a Christmas carol was sung and the children marched in to supper. A star-shaped table had been arranged for the occasion. In its centre was a small but handsomely decorated tree. The refreshments consisted of turkey sandwiches, cocoa, lemon jelly with whipped cream, sponge cake, bonbons and nuts. The sponge cake was baked in small star-shaped pans, and ornamented with red and white icing.

In the parlour an immense snowball was hung from the chandelier. This had been made by fastening four barrel-hoops

From Punch *1909*

FIRST YOUTH (*late arrival*): '*Hallo! What sort of show is it?*'
SECOND YOUTH: '*Oh, same old thing. First the dear old conjuror, and now the bally old Christmas tree!*'

together so as to form a round frame, over which was sewed white cambric. Then the ball was covered with batting and sprinkled with diamond dust. A slit was made in one side, and each child put in his hand and drew out some article wrapped in tissue paper. These proved to be dolls, balls and toys of all sorts. Some drew out tiny boxes inside of which were slips of paper with directions like these: 'Look under the divan and you will find a steam-engine,' 'Look beside the radiator and you will find a doll's kitchen,' etc. ■

CHRISTMAS UMBRELLA GAME

Take a large umbrella – an old one will do – wind the handle with bright yellow ribbon and line the body with red percaline as near the colour of holly berries as possible. Be sure to shape the lining so that it will not sag. Cover the outside with green percaline and finish the top with sprigs of holly and a bow of red and green ribbon. Trim the edge of the umbrella with a row of tiny bells and wind the ribs with crêpe or tissue paper the same colour as the lining; do this the last thing so that it will not come undone.

Select small appropriate gifts for the young guests; conceal them within dainty wrappings and tie them with ribbon to the ribs of the umbrella. When ready for the game let the children form a circle and choose one of their number to stand in the centre and hold the umbrella. The children may then dance around singing:

'*Merrily 'round this*
  Christmas ring,
Dancing gayly as we sing.
What would this umbrella
  bring
If we changed to hippetty-hop
And our hostess called out
  "*stop*"?'

When singing 'hippetty-hop' let the children hop around instead of dancing, and when the hostess calls out 'stop' the child with the umbrella raises it over his head and the present which sways longest belongs to him. He unties it, and as he does so he hands the umbrella to another child, whose place he takes in the circle, and so on until all the children have had a chance to hold the umbrella and receive one of the gifts which hang from it. After the game the umbrella may be given to the child who receives the largest number of votes as a souvenir of the evening.

If one does not wish the trouble of trimming an umbrella as described above, a Japanese umbrella may be purchased for a small sum, and will be equally appropriate. ■

MRS HERBERT B. LINSCOTT,
BRIGHT IDEAS FOR ENTERTAINING

'Snapdragon' was the most thrilling of all games, involving an element of danger and excitement. Traditionally played by the whole family on Christmas Eve it involved plucking from a bowl raisins that had been doused with brandy and then set alight. As eager but nervous fingers stretched towards the flames everyone would chant the following:

'Here he comes with flaming bowl, don't he meant to take his toll. Snip! Snap! Dragon. Take care you don't take too much. Be not greedy in your clutch.'

PUNCH, 9 JANUARY 1907

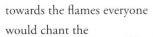

Eddie J. Andrews, Snapdragon

CHILDREN'S CHRISTMAS TABLEAUX

Build a cave-shaped box on a raised platform, drape inside and out with white muslin, fasten evergreen boughs about the entrance and at the back, draping all of these with loose tufts of cotton like new-fallen snow, and sprinkling them with mica. Sprays of red berries can be introduced with splendid effect. White covered steps must lead up to the cave, about the mouth of which may be spread white fur rugs. Let the candles be fastened plentifully around the cave, but have the rest of the room very dimly lighted. In the cave arrange the gifts, wrapped and properly marked, being careful to have one for each person present. Dress a pretty, golden-haired little girl as a fairy, with wings and spangles to enter the cave and bring out the gifts, and a couple of little boys as imps or brownies to deliver them. Low music should be played in some concealed corner, with now and again a song or chorus by a band of children dressed as fairies. The presentation of the tableaux may either precede or follow the distribution of the gifts.

Cinderella: A little girl, with torn calico dress and unkempt hair, stands at the right of the stage, her hands clasped and uplifted, smiling in wonder. Before her stands a very small boy in a smart military suit, with a white cotton wig on his head, indicating the coach in which she is to go to the ball. The coach may be a pumpkin hollowed into the proper shape, and drawn by a small dog, harnessed to it with ribbons, or a go-cart, or baby carriage, drawn by a larger dog. Someone behind the scenes plays a waltz very softly. Plenty of red fire.

Following the Flag: In one corner of the stage a tent is erected – a white sheet over a centre pole. All the small boys who have military suits, drums, trumpets and muskets, stand about, and one in the very front holds the flag. In front of the tent, on a pile of hay, lies another small boy, in a military suit, with his eyes closed, and behind him stands a little girl in a big white apron, with the symbol of the red cross on her left arm. Music behind the scenes is either 'Tenting on the Old Camp Ground', or 'The Star Spangled Banner', and all the rest of the red fire is ignited. When it dies down, the curtain is drawn, the lights are turned up, and the pianist plays 'Home, Sweet Home'. ■

MRS HERBERT B. LINSCOTT,
BRIGHT IDEAS FOR ENTERTAINING

From Punch *1907*: Uncle Showing Children How to Act

DUMB CRAMBO

Half the company leave the room. While they are absent, the others fix on a verb which the absent ones are to guess and perform. By and bye, when their decision is made, they call in the leader of the outside party, and say, 'The verb we have chosen for you rhymes with *pie*' (or any other word chosen). The leader retires, and discusses with her followers what the verb can be. It is best to take those which will rhyme with the noun given, in alphabetical order. 'Buy' would come first for 'Pie'. The party enter and begin to buy of each other. If right (that is, if 'to buy' was the word chosen), the spectators clap their hands; if wrong, they hiss. Speech on either side would entail a forfeit. If hissed, the actors retire, and arrange what next to do. 'Cry' would be the next rhyme, or 'dye' or 'eye' or 'fly', or 'hie', or 'sigh', or 'tie', all of which are acted in turn, till the clap of approval announces that the guess is a successful one. Then the spectators go out, and become in their turn actors, in the same manner. A great deal of the fun of this game depends on the acting and on the choice of the verbs; but it is almost sure to cause great amusement. ■

THE GIRL'S HOME COMPANION

The anticipation of and preparation for a party all too often proves more exciting than the event itself, as the young Dodie Smith found to her chagrin – even though it included kissing games.

By the Christmas of 1904 I was a fully-fledged party-goer. The invitations, with fancy decorations, usually said, 'We are giving a little party and should so much like to see you there.' If, at the bottom, was '3 till 8 o'clock' it was a babies' party. '4 to 9' was better and '5 to 10' was bliss. And there were a few glorious invitations on plain gilt-edged cards which said 'Dancing, 6 to 11'. I was never allowed to stay till eleven, but even to possess one of these almost grown-up cards made one feel mature.

The thrill of a party began the night before when my mother took special care over putting my hair in curl-rags. Every curl that was not quite tight enough was done again and I did not complain if the tightness was uncomfortable, it was part of the excitement. I cannot now imagine how I managed to sleep with those hard knobs, like glossy chestnuts from each of which sprouted a flutter of white curl-rag, all over my head. Next day time hung heavily until the afternoon when, on being told by my mother that everything was ready, I would steal upstairs, open the bedroom door very quietly, and gloat. The fire would be burning brightly and on the bed would be my party dress (always pink chiffon), a pink cloth hooded cape, a white wool shawl to go over it, bronze slippers, white silk openwork stockings, white silk mittens and a choice of three fans – ostrich feather, hand-painted, or lace. On the dressing-table white corals, a very small diamond heart on a pink ribbon and a pearl-set swastika on a narrow golden chain awaited my selection . . .

To this day, the smell of tangerines brings back memories of those disillusioning parties: the drawing-room cleared for games with the chairs set round the walls – tidy to start with but gradually becoming littered with paper caps and pulled crackers; the Christmas tree with burnt-out candles – never did I get a present that pleased me; the huge tea where nothing tasted as good as it looked; my desperate effort to enjoy myself which gradually changed to flat disappointment. Other children seemed blissfully happy – but *I* must have *seemed* happy; I romped and shouted and never ceased to smile, more to encourage myself than out of politeness . . .

From Punch *1907*

HOSTESS: *'Goodbye, darling. So sorry Nurse has come for you. I hope you and Monty have enjoyed yourselves?'*

DARLING: *'Thank you. Mother says we've enjoyed ourselves very much!'*

During the first hours of parties there were boisterous games such as 'Hunt the Slipper', 'Blind Man's Buff', 'Nuts in May' – game of ignominy for me as children far smaller than I was could pull me across; but after tea there were kissing games, 'Shy Widow', 'Turn and Trencher' and, most popular of all, 'Postman's Knock'. I was chosen often enough by little boys, but never did glorious young men of thirteen or fourteen thump on the door and demand my presence in the hall, where the lights were turned low and giggling maids hid in dim kitchen passages to watch the fun. ■

DODIE SMITH, *LOOK BACK WITH LOVE*

Sir Alfred Munnings, Advertisement for Crackers

REGINALD'S CHRISTMAS REVEL

On Christmas evening, we were supposed to be specially festive in the Old English fashion. The hall was horribly draughty, but it seemed to be the proper place to revel in, and it was decorated with Japanese fans and Chinese lanterns which gave it a very Old English effect. A young lady with a confidential voice favoured us with a long recitation about a little girl who died or did something equally hackneyed, and then the Major gave us a graphic account of a struggle he had with a wounded bear. I privately wished that the bears would win some-times on these occasions; at least they wouldn't go vapouring about it after-wards. Before we had time to recover our spirits, we were indulged with some thought-reading by a young man whom one knew instinctively had a good mother and an indifferent tailor – the sort of young man who talks unflag-gingly through the thickest soup, and smooths his hair dubiously as though he thought it might hit back. The thought-reading was rather a success; he announced that the hostess was thinking about poetry, and she admitted that her mind was dwelling on one of Austin's odes. Which was near enough. I fancy she had really been wondering whether a scrag-end of mutton and some cold plum pudding would do for the kitchen dinner next day. As a crowning dis-sipation, they all sat down to play pro-gressive halma, with milk chocolate for prizes. I've been carefully brought up, and I don't like to play games of skill for milk chocolate, so I invented a headache and retired from the scene. I had been preceded a few minutes earlier by Miss Langshan-Smith, a rather formidable lady, who always got up at some uncomfortable hour in the morning, and gave you the impression that she had been in communication with most of the European Governments before breakfast.

Anon, Christmas Crackers

There was a paper pinned on her door with a signed request that she might be called particularly early on the morrow. Such an opportunity does not come twice in a lifetime. I covered up everything except the signature with another notice, to the effect that before these words should meet the eye she would have ended a misspent life, was sorry for the trouble she was giving, and would like a military funeral. A few minutes later I violently exploded an air-filled paper bag on the landing, and gave a stage moan that could have been heard in the cellars. Then I pursued my original intention and went to bed. The noise those people made in forcing open the good lady's door was positively indecorous; she resisted gallantly, but I believe they searched her for bullets for about a quarter of an hour, as if she had been a historic battlefield.

I hate travelling on Boxing Day, but one must occasionally do things that one dislikes. ■

SAKI (H.H. MUNRO),
REGINALD'S CHRISTMAS REVEL

What would a Christmas party be without its grand finale of cracker pulling? We have to thank for this Tom Smith, a young baker who was initially inspired by the French habit of wrapping bonbons in coloured paper with twisted ends. To give his sweets new appeal Tom added a tiny explosive charge to the wrapping in the form of a chemically treated strip of card. To sustain the momentum in sales and appeal to a wider market, he later added hats, mottoes, riddles and novelties. By the early 1900s he was selling millions all over the world and the cracker had become an established part of Christmas.

Anon, At Home

Gathering around the piano to sing both topical or familiar old songs usually brought out the best in everyone and a jolly time would be had by all. The following is an old music hall song, the 'halls' being a colourful and most popular feature of Edwardian life. Cheap and always cheerful, the entertainment on offer was a lively mix of jugglers, conjurors, soubrettes like Marie Lloyd, 'male impersonators' such as Vesta Tilley and comedians like Little Tich, Grock and Harry Tate. The songs heard would later be whistled in the streets or sung around the piano at home.

BEST WISHES

UNDER THE MISTLETOE

A grand and jolly old custom you will find at Christmas time
In every house you go, hangs the bunch of mistletoe
You find it hanging upon the wall and every charming Miss
She's always hovering round it for a kiss
At first you kiss the Master, then the daughters, three or four
And then you kiss the maiden aunt who's never been kissed before.

Under the Mistletoe – O, Under the Mistletoe
Young maids, old maids, dearly love to go
Oh! did you ever, ever hear a girl say 'No'
When you whisper 'Come and kiss me under the Mistletoe?' – toe.

The sweet and spooney young couple, oh! they quite enjoy the fun.
They wander to and fro, underneath the mistletoe:
And when the couple are man and wife the following Christmastide,
Before them all he'll boldly kiss the bride.
Another Christmas Day comes round, and then the happy pair,
They're at the same old game, and now they're kissing a son and heir
Under the Mistletoe, etc.

Now, there's the grumpy old bach'lor who's in digging all alone,
The servant gives a grin as she brings the turkey in;
A feeling then overcomes him he has seldom felt before,
He sees the mistletoe above the door.
He gives the girl a Christmas box, then steals a kiss with glee:
It's only once a year, of course he likes it and so does she.
Under the Mistletoe, etc.

The sweet kiss under the mistletoe will always be the thing,
It gives the modest miss excuses for a kiss;
You kiss her under the parlour stairs, her dignity she'll show,
She likes it underneath the mistletoe.
A bunch of mistletoe's the thing to bring you perfect bliss –
I always carry some myself [produce Mistletoe] – would anyone like a kiss?
Under the Mistletoe, etc.

WORDS AND MUSIC BY A.J. MILLS AND HARRY CASTLING

OPPOSITE: *Anon,* Mistletoe

Amateur dramatists and aspiring young playwrights in a family would conjure up a drama to be performed over Christmas. All that was needed was a lively imagination, an outgoing nature, a bulging dressing-up box and, of course, an appreciative audience who would tolerate any shortcomings.

From the far beginnings of 'Dumb Crambo' and 'Charades', we gradually climbed to the heights of the Christmas play. This was written in committee, by us all together, and was the principal event of the year. As soon as one play was acted we instantly began planning the next one, even upon Boxing Day! They were performed in our house, on the evening of Christmas Day, and were followed by the Christmas dinner, which was attended by all the family then in Cambridge, and by no one else at all.

These plays were built up on a good solid foundation of Gilbert and Sullivan, and were full of topical allusions. They always had a chorus, in which we all took part, whenever we were not on the stage in some other capacity, because we were short of actors. Bernard wrote and recited the Prologue, but he was too grown-up to act with us; Erasmus disliked acting and refused to take part. Charles probably disliked it quite as much, but public opinion always compelled him to be the Prince and to wear the beautiful Russian boots – a present from Felix – which were the Prince's insignia, and the glory of our dressing-up box. Nora was considered the prettiest of us (to her disgust), so she generally had to be the Princess, which was very dull for her. Ruth and Margaret were celebrated actresses and had character parts; and the rest of us were Witches, Professors, Ghosts or whatever was required. I did a good deal of the costume designing, and used to cut out dresses by the simple process of laying the patient down on a piece of butter muslin, and cutting out round his edges. But we had a pretty good stock of curious cast-off odds and ends to fall back on. There was no scenery, and only a screen for a curtain. The plots were incredibly complicated; no one really understood them; but

Percy Tarrant, Christmas Fancy Dress Party

that was no matter; for the success of the play depended entirely on the wit, and the verses. The dialogue was in prose, and full of jokes . . .

As we grew older the plays grew more informal, but we still always acted some half-impromptu skit on Christmas Day. ∎

GWEN RAVERAT, *PERIOD PIECE*

'Charades' was *the* game to play and the following advice on how to play it comes from *Enquire Within upon Everything*. Published in 1896 this marvellous little book gave advice on things as various as choosing fresh fish for the table to the best way to clean ostrich feathers.

Charades: A drawing-room with folded doors is the best for the purpose. Various household appliances are employed to fit up something like a stage, and to supply the fitting scenes. Characters dressed in costumes made up of handkerchiefs, coats, shawls, table-covers, etc., come on and perform an extempore play, founded upon the parts of a word, and its *whole*. For instance if one chose the word *ear-ring*, in the first act glasses might be rung for bells – something might be said in the course of the dialogue about the sound of the bells being delightful to the *ear*, then there might be a dance of the villagers, in which a *ring* might be formed or a wedding might be performed; the final act must include the whole word. ■

ENQUIRE WITHIN UPON EVERYTHING

J.B. Priestley captures the unpretentious fun of the Edwardian Christmases of his youth which relied on good company rather than lavish sums of money being spent.

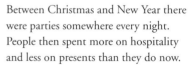

Between Christmas and New Year there were parties somewhere every night. People then spent more on hospitality and less on presents than they do now.

I remember uproarious parties, when I laughed myself into a red haze at 'Charades'.

J.B. PRIESTLEY, *THE EDWARDIANS*

The richness of the Edwardian pantomime was matched only by that of the Victorian, the period during which it became an institution for all the family. The early pantomimes in the eighteenth century featured *commedia dell'arte* characters such as Harlequin, Columbine and Mr Punch and were an excuse to produce extraordinary stage effects, transformation scenes being the most popular. All these elements survived to a greater or lesser degree, as Ernest Shepard stands witness, but much else was added. Figures such as Aladdin and Cinderella took over the major roles and the panto became a marvellous *mélange* of music hall turns interwoven into the telling of a familiar children's story. It was, as Shepard says, 'a feast of colour, music and fun'.

F.D. Bedford, At Drury Lane

Then the curtain rose and I became lost to all around me, translated to another land, borne aloft on magic wings into another world.

The story must have been *The Babes in the Wood*, for otherwise why should Harry Nicholls and Herbert Campbell, both outsize Babes, have appeared seated side by side in an enormous double perambulator and proceeded to sing a duet?

Two bandits, though hired for the purpose of making away with this innocent pair, spent most of their energies in knockabout comedy. Can they have been the Griffiths brothers, the famous inventors of Pogo the horse? The scene in the kitchen of the wicked Baron's house was a riot below stairs, with a cat who jumped over a large kitchen table, all laid ready for a meal; he jumped like a real animal and landed on his forelegs, a thing no one but Charles Laurie could do. This was before Dan Leno's day; he did not come to Drury Lane till a year or two later. But I remember a gay young woman with prominent teeth and a flaxen wig who sang and danced bewitchingly. She could only have been Marie Lloyd, the unforgettable, aged seventeen and in her first Pantomime at 'the Lane'. In the Harlequinade the clown was an old favourite, Harry Payne, so Father told us, who had been clowning for years and was shortly to give place to another famous clown, Whimsical Walker.

It was all such a feast of colour, music and fun, and it would be quite impossible to express all the emotions that were aroused in a small boy's breast. I know that I stood gripping the velvet-coloured front of the box, lost in a wonderful dream, and that when the curtain fell at the end of the first act and the lights in the auditorium went up, I sat back on Mother's lap with a sigh. I could not speak when she asked me if I was enjoying the show. I could only nod my head. I did not think it possible that such feminine charms existed as were displayed by the Principal Boy. Ample-bosomed, small-waisted and with thighs – oh, such thighs! – thighs that shone and glittered in the different coloured silk tights in which she continually appeared. How she strode about the stage, proud and dominant, smacking those rounded limbs with a riding crop! At every smack, a fresh dart was shot into the heart of at least one young adorer. I had a grand feeling that it was all being done for my especial benefit: the whole performance was for *me*; the cast had all been told that they were to do their best because *I* was there. Nobody else, not even Mother, could feel exactly the same as I did.

The spectacle reached a climax with the transformation scene. Glittering vistas appeared one behind the other, sparkling lace-like canopies spread overhead, a real fountain poured forth in the background. On either side golden brackets swung out from the wings, each with its reclining nymph, solid and spangled and in a graceful attitude. Flying fairies, poised but swaying gently, filled the air and formed a sort of triumphal archway, below which the performers gathered. The Good Fairy, stepping forward, invoked in rhymed couplets the Spirit of Pantomime, and out from the wings burst Joey the clown, Pantaloon, Columbine, and Harlequin to complete the tableau. Not quite, for, led by the Principal Boy, there came Augustus Harris himself, immaculate in evening dress with white waistcoat, to receive the plaudits of a delighted audience.

There was still the Harlequinade to come. The red-hot poker (that kept hot for a remarkably long time), the strings of sausages, the stolen goose, the Pantaloon always in difficulties, the Policeman, blown up and put together again. Oh, how I longed for it to go on for ever! Then Harlequin, with a wave of his wand, brought on his Columbine, so fair and dainty, but not so lovely as to steal one's heart, though she helped Joey to rob the shopman. On came the tall thin man who sang and sang the while he was belaboured by Joey and Pantaloon. And then – the end! ■

ERNEST H. SHEPARD, *DRAWN FROM MEMORY*

J.M. Barrie's *Peter Pan* – now a Christmas classic – was first performed in December 1904. Mostly the reviewers praised it:

> '**Peter Pan** *is from beginning to end a thing of pure delight.*'
> A.B. WALKLEY, *THE TIMES*

The one play of the month which stands out conspicuously above the other productions, whether written for children or grown-up children, is the most fantastic work that the most fantastic of our playwrights has hitherto attempted. *Peter Pan; or, The Boy who wouldn't Grow Up*, at the Duke of York's, possesses the double claim of appealing both to young boys and maidens, old men and matrons, and to all who have not yet lost either their sense of humour or that child-like half-belief in fairies and creatures born of a pure imagination. It is not so easy a thing nowadays to write a play that will be applauded by an average London audience. It is still more difficult to do so when the audience is composed of men and women of the world and clever wide-awake children home for the holidays, and therefore expecting much: but Mr J.M. Barrie has succeeded twice over.

Peter Pan is charming because it is original as well as fantastic, and because there is a humorous and happy blend of the mystical and the real . . . It is just this spirit which makes grandparents laugh, and which kills at one blow the remark which the very modern matter-of-fact schoolboy is waiting to utter. He cannot say, 'What awful rot! No one ever believes in fairy-tales nowadays,' because that is precisely the utterance Mr Barrie anticipates. ∎

    E. KEBLE CHATTERTON, *THE LADY'S REALM*

But not all were so enthusiastic: 'Oh, for an hour of Herod!' yelped the writer Anthony Hope, whose pain was echoed by George Bernard Shaw, who mistakenly judged that it was an entertainment 'foisted on children by the grown-ups'. But childless himself, he had doubtless forgotten a child's need for and enjoyment of fantasy.

Sigismund de Ivanowski, Maude Adams in a Stage Version of *Peter Pan*

Augustus E. Mulready, Remembering Joys that Have Passed Away

Undoubtedly, *Peter Pan* is the best thing [Barrie] has done – the thing most directly from within himself. Here, at last we see his talent in its full maturity; for here he has stripped off from himself the last flimsy remnants of a pretence to maturity . . .

Mr Barrie is not that rare creature, a man of genius. He is something even more rare – a child who, by some divine grace, can express through an artistic medium the childishness that is in him . . . Mr Barrie has never grown up.

MAX BEERBOHM,
THE SATURDAY REVIEW

MERRY JEST CHRISTMAS CRACKERS WITH RIBBONS

Why not match Tom Smith's elaborate and exciting crackers with your own and have some fun making up riddles to go inside them?

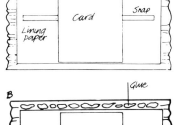

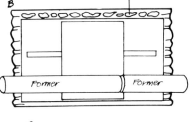

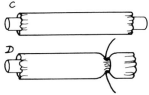

Measurements
Length 12in (30.5cm)

Materials for 1 cracker
Single crêpe paper
6¾in × 12in (17cm × 30.5cm)
Lining paper
6in × 11in (5cm × 28cm)
One snap
One motto
3½in × 6in (9cm × 15cm) Stiffener
card (flexible, lightweight card)
Uhu adhesive
Two formers: one 5in (12.5cm) long
and one 10in (25cm) long, both
with approximately 1½in (3.75cm)
diameter. (Use bought formers or
use plastic piping from builders'
merchants. Formers can also be
made by rolling stiff card and
securing with Sellotape.)
Thin twine
One gift
Selection of Offray ribbons

To Make
1 Frill short ends of crêpe paper by pulling between fingers to stretch.

2 Lay crêpe paper on table. Put lining paper on top with bottom edges level.
3 Lay snap and motto across lining paper. Lay card centrally on lining paper with bottom edge level (A).
4 Spread glue thinly across top edge of crêpe paper.
5 Lay the large former across the card stiffener, 1in (2.5cm) from bottom edge of cracker papers. The right-hand edge should line up with the right-hand edge of the card (B).
6 Lay the smaller former on the right-hand end of the larger former, just touching (B).
7 Now start to roll the cracker up from the bottom, keeping the formers in position. Roll firmly and then press the cracker down on to the glued edge to secure. Hold until the glue dries.
8 Carefully withdraw the small former from the right-hand end, about 2in (5cm) (C). Wrap the piece of twine carefully around the cracker, at point of edge of stiffener card. Pull the twine tight and remove small former. This will give the cracker a 'waisted' shape (D).

9 Pull the larger former out from the other end until it is 2in (5cm) away from the left-hand end of the stiffener card inside the cracker. Insert gift. Use the twine as before to make the waist. (If preferred make the waist more defined afterwards by tying a piece of matching thread around tightly.)
10 Glue Offray ribbons around the cracker ends just above the frilled edge. Decorate the cracker with lace and further ribbons, taking care to choose colours which will complement the shade of the crêpe paper. ■

ACKNOWLEDGEMENTS

AUTHOR'S ACKNOWLEDGEMENTS

My thanks to the following who have helped me with research and lent me precious copies of Edwardian books and magazines: Tessa Barnford, Maggie Black, Kate Dyson, Lamorna Good, Marnie Gribbin, Monica Jennings, Nicky Manisty, Phil Murray, Charles Orme, George Radford and Caroline Weeks. My thanks also to Delian Bower for his advice on compiling the book and to my incredibly efficient and encouraging editor, Anne Askwith.

The author and publisher gratefully acknowledge the following for permission to reproduce extracts in this book:

page 134 Gwen Raverat, *Period Piece*, Faber & Faber Ltd;
128 Dodie Smith, *Look Back with Love*, Film Rights Ltd;
135 J. B. Priestley, *The Edwardians*, Rainbird 1970, copyright © J. B. Priestley 1970;
46, 137 E. H. Shepard, *Drawn from Memory*, Methuen London Ltd., copyright © E. H. Shepard 1957 and in the US copyright © 1957 by E. H. Shepard, renewed © 1985 by Mary Knox;
73 Eugene Frazer, *The House by the Dvina*, Mainstream Publishing Co.;
27 extract from *Vita Sackville-West's Garden Book* reproduced by permission of Curtis Brown, London, on behalf of the author's estate;

24 from *The Garden* © 1946 Vita Sackville-West, reproduced by permission of Curtis Brown, London, on behalf of the author's estate;

15 Virginia Woolf, *The Flight of the Mind*, Letters 1888–1912, ed. N. Nicolson and J. Trautmann, The Hogarth Press, reproduced by permission of the Executors of the Virginia Woolf Estate;

35 John Betjeman, *Collected Poems*, John Murray (Publishers) Ltd;

104, 105 the Executors of the Estate of Elizabeth Yandell and the Bodley Head for extracts from *Henry*;

Anon, Boy and Girl Pulling a Cracker

68 The Literary Trustees of Walter de la Mare and the Society of Authors as their representative;

97 The Society of Authors on behalf of the Bernard Shaw Estate.

The following extracts are from the series of *Country Diary* books published by Webb & Bower/Michael Joseph Ltd:

page 78 Sid Sykes, *The Country Diary Book of Decorating*;

59, 62, 63, 79, 80 Carol Petelin, *The Country Diary Book of Flowers*;

60, 70, 89, 140 Annette Mitchell, *The Country Diary Book of Crafts*;

29, 30, 82 Annette Mitchell, *The Country Diary Book of Knitting*;

32, 115 Sarah Hollis, *The Country Diary Herbal*;

76 Rowena Stott, *The Country Diary Book of Stencilling.*

89, 95, 99, 108, 109, 111 Alison Harding, *The Country Diary Cookery Notes.*

ILLUSTRATIONS

page 7 Mr K. C. T. Palmer;

10 Copyright © Frederick Warne & Co., 1971, 19 Copyright © Frederick Warne & Co., 1978;

14 (Musée d'Orsay) and 88 (Musée des Beaux-Arts, Tourcoing) (Giraudon), 18 (Roy Miles Gallery), 23 (private collection), 26 (Cassell & Co Ltd., London), 36 (Osterreichische Nationalbibliothek, Vienna), 44 (private collection), 45 (private collection), 46 (Hirsch Sprungske Coll.), 47 and 50 (by courtesy of the Board of Trustees of the Victoria and Albert Museum), 48 above (private collection), 48 below (private collection), 49 above left (private collection), 52 (private collection), 58 below (private collection), 67 (private collection), 70 (private collection), 71 (Chris Beetles Ltd., London), 72 (private collection), 74 (City of Bristol Museum & Art Gallery), 98 (from the collection of Worthing Museum & Art Gallery), 101 (private collection), 104 (Christopher Wood Gallery), 106 (Anthony Crane Collection), 118 and 120 (Library of Congress, Washington D.C.), 124 (private collection), 129 (by courtesy of the Board of Trustees of the Victoria and Albert Museum, copyright the Sir Alfred Munnings Art Museum), 138 (Guildhall Art Gallery, Corporation of London) Bridgeman Art Library;

17, 21, 40, 42, 43, 51, 53, 54, 68, 86, 93, 94, 97, 100, 103, 112, 117 (above), 127, 130, 131, 133, 136, 139, 142 Mary Evans Picture Library;

20 Tate Gallery, London;

25 lent by Rowena Stott;

28 lent by Ina Taylor;

29, 30, 82 from *The Country Diary Book of Knitting*;

32, 114 Simon McBride, from *The Country Diary Herbal*;

34 Norfolk Museums Service (Norwich Castle Museum);

3, 38, 48, 49, 134 Fine Art Photographic Library Ltd;

57 *Illustrated London News*;

58 (above), 107, 122 (left), 132 (left), 165 from a private Edwardian scrapbook;

59, 62, 63, 78, 80, 81 Simon McBride, from *The Country Diary Book of Flowers*;

61, 77, 84, 140 from *The Country Diary Book of Crafts*;

76 Charles Parsons, from *The Country Diary Book of Stencilling*;

78 (left) from *The Country Diary Book of Decorating*;

89 (above), 90–91, 96, 99, 105 (above), 110–111 (above), 113 from *Book of Household Management* by Mrs Beeton;

128 from *Punch* 1907;

102 from *Punch* 1908;

125, 127 from *Punch* 1909;

110–111 (below) from *The Ladies' Field*, 1913;

117 from *Mr Punch's Book of Sports*;

121, 123 from *The Games Book for Boys and Girls*;

138 (left) from *The Lady's Realm* 1905.

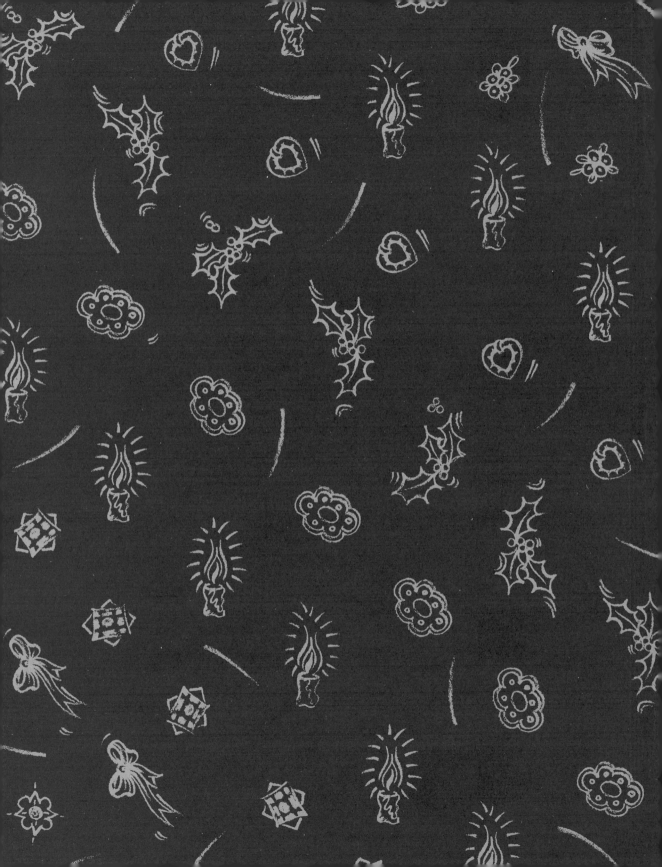